D0110792

PRAISE FOR
Squeeze the Moment

The touching and encouraging stories in *Squeeze the Moment* renewed my passion for turning daily events—and challenges—into lifelong memories. Like a light switch flipping on in our hearts, Karen O'Connor illuminates the joy found in purposeful living and brightens our desire to nurture relationships with family and friends. A great book to read and share!

TRICIA GOYER
AWARD-WINNING AUTHOR, *LIFE INTERRUPTED: THE SCOOP ON BEING A YOUNG MOM*

Illustrated with heart-warming stories, *Squeeze the Moment* demonstrates seven deceptively simple (yet powerful) principles for living with joy. Karen lives what she teaches, and her action steps help the reader put the principles into practice. The short chapters make this book perfect for busy people looking to put the joy back into living.

KRISTI HOLL
AUTHOR, *NO BOYS ALLOWED* AND *GIRLZ ROCK*

Karen O'Connor is a remarkable writer and speaker. With humor, inspiration, stories from real life and practical applications for living a purposeful life, she grips the attention of her readers and her audiences. Her books have hit a hot button and I highly recommend her latest work, *Squeeze the Moment*. Buy one for yourself and 10 more to give away.

CAROL KENT
SPEAKER, SPEAK UP SPEAKER SERVICES
AUTHOR, *WHEN I LAY MY ISAAC DOWN*

If you wish you could add another hour to your day, this is the book for you! If you don't have time to read another book about time management, then do yourself a favor and make this book your top priority. This book is not just another time management book—it's a life management book. Karen O'Connor is not about guilt—she's all about pleasure and how to enjoy the everyday moments in life. Ever feel like you're just working your way through life? *Squeeze the Moment* will multiply your time by showing you how to redeem your attitude. Does it feel like your life has lost all its promise? *Squeeze the Moment* will help you rediscover it.

SIRI L. MITCHELL
AUTHOR, *KISSING ADRIEN*

Gifted author Karen O'Connor shares seven simple and soul-searching secrets for *intentional* living. Through her heartwarming, healing and helpful stories, you'll learn how to soak up life's joy, squeeze all its wonder and fill your heart to overflowing again with God's love. I highly recommend *Squeeze the Moment*. What a wonderful book!

LYNN D. MORRISSEY
AUTHOR, *LOVE LETTERS TO GOD*
SPEAKER, AWSA/CLASS

Karen O'Connor is a special writer who knows how to turn our hearts to the Lord in practical and thoughtful ways. I recommend her!

GAYLE ROPER
AUTHOR, *ALLAH'S FIRE* AND THE SEASIDE SEASONS SERIES
SPEAKER, GAYLE ROPER MINISTRIES

A treasure! *Squeeze the Moment* will delight, surprise, encourage and uplift you. A wonderful way to start your day!

CYNDY SALZMANN
AUTHOR, *MAKING YOUR HOME A HAVEN* AND
THE FRIDAY AFTERNOON CLUB MYSTERY SERIES
SPEAKER, FAMILY HAVEN MINISTRIES

squeeze
the
moment

Karen O'Connor

Regal

From Gospel Light
Ventura, California, U.S.A.

PUBLISHED BY REGAL BOOKS
FROM GOSPEL LIGHT
VENTURA, CALIFORNIA, U.S.A.
Regal   PRINTED IN THE U.S.A.

Regal Books is a ministry of Gospel Light, a Christian publisher dedicated to serving the local church. We believe God's vision for Gospel Light is to provide church leaders with biblical, user-friendly materials that will help them evangelize, disciple and minister to children, youth and families.

It is our prayer that this Regal book will help you discover biblical truth for your own life and help you meet the needs of others. May God richly bless you.

For a free catalog of resources from Regal Books/Gospel Light, please call your Christian supplier or contact us at 1-800-4-GOSPEL *or* www.regalbooks.com.

Library of Congress Cataloging-in-Publication Data
O'Connor, Karen, 1938-
  Squeeze the moment : making the most of life's gifts and challenges / Karen O'Connor.—
[New ed.].
    p. cm.
  ISBN 0-8307-3836-3 (trade paper)
  1. Christian life. I. Title.

BV4501.3.O325 2006
242'.2—dc22   2005030924

1   2   3   4   5   6   7   8   9   10   /   10   09   08   07   06

Rights for publishing this book in other languages are contracted by Gospel Light Worldwide, the international nonprofit ministry of Gospel Light. Gospel Light Worldwide also provides publishing and technical assistance to international publishers dedicated to producing Sunday School and Vacation Bible School curricula and books in the languages of the world. For additional information, visit www.gospellightworldwide.org; write to Gospel Light Worldwide, P.O. Box 3875, Ventura, CA 93006; or send an e-mail to info@gospellightworldwide.org.

*Dedicated to the memory of
my mother, Eva.*

*To my sisters,
June and Shevawn,
and to my daughters,
Julie and Erin,*

with love and a grateful heart.

Contents

Precept Four: Do a Physical Exercise

Precept Five: Do a Mental Exercise

Precept Six: Look for Joy in Unexpected Places

Precept Seven: End Each Day with an Original Prayer of Thanks

Introduction

While leafing through an issue of *Reader's Digest* some years ago, an article entitled "Lessons from Aunt Grace" caught my attention. The author, Nardi Reeder Campion, described a time in her life when she felt depressed—even hopeless—until one day she discovered an old diary kept by a maiden aunt 40 years before. Frail, poor and alone, Campion's Aunt Grace had to depend on relatives for her living.

"I know I must be cheerful," she wrote, "living in this large family upon whom I am dependent. Yet gloom haunts me. Clearly my situation is not going to change; therefore, *I* shall have to change."[1]

According to her diary entry, Aunt Grace resolved to do six things each day in order to hold her world together: do something for someone else, do something for herself, do something she didn't want to do that needed doing, do a physical exercise, do a mental exercise, and end each day with an original prayer that included counting her blessings. The rest of the article describes how these six precepts helped change the author's life, just as they had changed Aunt Grace's life decades before.

"Can life be lived by a formula?" asks the author. "All I know," she replies, "is that since I started to live by those six precepts, I've become more involved with others, and hence, less buried in myself." And she learned to follow her aunt's motto: Bloom where you are planted.[2]

I was heartened by what I read. *If such actions worked for these women*, I thought, *maybe they could work for me*. I was facing some tough times myself, recovering from a divorce, adjusting to a new marriage, relocating to a new city and being separated from some of my family, good friends and familiar surroundings. I needed more than just encouraging words.

At the same time, I didn't want to cram another set of rules into my life. I had had enough "should" systems, self-help seminars and feel-better workshops. What I wanted was more freedom, more joy, more spontaneity.

I began tentatively, wondering if such simple steps could really work. I didn't practice them in any particular order, and I didn't do each one every day. I considered them *reminders* rather than *rules*—there to help me seize the moment and make the most of it, as Aunt Grace appeared to have done.

Little by little, I noticed subtle changes occur. For example, when I took time to do something for myself as well as for others I had more energy for physical exercise. Walking, swimming, hiking in the mountains or taking care of my plants helped clear my mind so that I was able to do a mental task without strain, which led to my being willing to do what needed doing—even when I didn't feel like it or want to—such as balancing my checkbook or taking my car in for an oil change or initiating a conversation with a difficult person.

At the end of each day, I found it easy to whisper a prayer of thanks. The precepts worked. As long as I was alert to life, practicing the precepts was easy. I didn't even have to think about them. How freeing!

The more I participated in life instead of simply passing through it, the more joy I felt. In fact, I began to find joy, even in unexpected places, such as the hospital room where my father died. I began waking up in the morning eager to live in the moment—whether jogging along the beach near my home, reading a chapter here and there of the many books I had bought but never read, praying spontaneously for someone, giving up my need to be right when my husband and I disagreed, working on my latest writing assignment without fretting, or cleaning behind the sofas even when I didn't feel like it!

I was waking up to life. Joy welled up inside me. The sunsets were now more beautiful to me than ever before. The birds in the tree outside our bedroom window seemed to sing just for me. Tasks I once dreaded, such as cleaning closets, purging files and returning phone calls were suddenly easier—even pleasant—because I was doing them with a heart of joy!

You, too, can experience joy and peace each day. I have written this book to encourage and inspire you to do just that by becoming more alert to life so that you can quickly recognize moments of opportunity, as Aunt Grace did, and so that you will feel eager and willing to squeeze those moments of every drop!

The purpose of the stories and suggestions on the following pages is to ignite a desire to respond without planning, to be at the ready, to move in the Spirit, to see a need and to act on it, to do good without constraint, even to experiment.

Think of Aunt Grace. She faced the challenge of living her last years totally dependent on relatives—the perfect setup for a pity party! Instead, she focused on joy by living in the moment, doing for others *as well as for herself*, exercising her mind and body, ticking off tasks she didn't particularly want to do but still doing them since they needed to be done, and closing each day with a prayer of thanksgiving.

I imagine that soon after she made this positive mental ascent, her precepts became such a part of her life that she didn't even have to think about them. She just *did* them. I hope this will happen for you, too. I hope that spontaneous joy will flow out of you naturally because you'll be drawn by the Spirit to do good things for yourself and others; then give thanks to God for all of it.

The book is divided into seven sections based on the six precepts from Aunt Grace and an additional one I've tucked in: *look for joy in unexpected places.*

Each section has a short introduction, several stories or essays to illustrate the theme or precept, appropriate Scriptures, one or two suggestions for how you can begin practicing these precepts in your own life starting now, a simple prayer and an inspirational quotation.

Make this your journey. If no one else in your life shares your enthusiasm, so be it. Maybe God is calling you to be an example in their lives. People who focus on joy, who look at life through its lens, and who express joy in all their dealings and relationships have a more satisfying life. What we set our minds and hearts to, we will experience.

I pray that you, too, will be motivated to look at your life in a fresh way and to *live* each moment—happy, tragic, expected, unexpected—for all its worth and to find the joy within each one in a way you've never had before, regardless of the circumstances.

Karen O'Connor
San Diego, California

Notes

1. Nardi Reeder Campion, "Lessons from Aunt Grace," *Reader's Digest*, vol. 125 (July 1984), p. 91. Emphasis in original.
2. Ibid.

Precept 1

Do Something for Someone Else

DO NOT WITHHOLD GOOD FROM THOSE WHO DESERVE IT,
WHEN IT IS IN YOUR POWER TO ACT.
PROVERBS 3:27

"HELLO!" you may be shouting at me. "That's my whole life—doing things for other people. I don't need to hear more about *this* one. In fact, you can skip it."

I understand. I agree with you. But I'm not talking about the usual fare: preparing meals, making beds, running kids from piano lessons to soccer practice, visiting your mother, writing a report, babysitting a neighbor's child, covering for a coworker who's out sick. You probably do all that and more, and you do it *well*. I'm referring here to the kinds of doing that hold an element of surprise, spontaneity, serendipity—the kinds of things that knock people's socks off. Doing something for someone you love or even for someone you don't know well, or at all, that will bring a moment of unbridled joy—the kind that will spill into your life as well.

That's what happens when we do something for someone else with intention and attention, as the stories on the following pages illustrate. You'll meet a woman who does something for her husband that blesses him—and her! A young woman learns about kindness from an older woman's spontaneous generosity in the laundry room, of all places! A mother realizes what her daughter really needs and gives it to her. Two women become "partners of the heart," blessing one another with daily prayer. A woman welcomes a new neighbor into the community with a gesture that is both caring and practical. And a woman discovers how to bless loved ones with heirloom jewelry.

A WIFE OF NOBLE CHARACTER WHO CAN FIND?
SHE IS WORTH FAR MORE THAN RUBIES.
PROVERBS 31:10

Roll in the Hay

"Kate, guess what Jerry gave me for Christmas?" Colleen asked her friend as they walked around the lake in their community one early morning. Kate noticed the excitement in Colleen's tone.

"I have no idea," Kate said, smiling. "But from the sound of your voice it must have been pretty special. A new car? A cruise? What? Now I'm really curious!"

"This," said Colleen, as she plucked a large shiny coin from her pocket and handed it to her friend. "Read the inscription," she said. "It's adorable."

"To Colleen, from Jerry," Kate read aloud.

"Turn it over," her friend urged, obviously eager to see Kate's reaction.

"Love token. Good for one roll in the hay!"

"Read the small lettering," Colleen prompted.

"No expiration date!" Kate burst out laughing. "This is adorable," she agreed, "especially coming from unassuming Jerry. What got into him?"

Colleen carried on, telling Kate that she and Jerry had lost the joy in their lovemaking. They seemed to be going through the motions without any passion. Maybe it was that way for lots of couples married more than 25 years, but they didn't like it.

"So Jerry decided to throw me a curve," said Colleen. "I was blown away."

Kate was dying to ask Colleen whether she had redeemed the token, but Kate decided not to go *that* far.

Colleen returned the token to her pocket, and the women continued their walk, moving on to other subjects such as aging parents, grandchildren, the latest movie and the upcoming women's retreat at their church.

After an hour of walking, they had broken a good sweat, hugged each other good-bye and went their separate ways. As Kate drove home, she noticed she was beginning to feel agitated and then jealous—jealous of Colleen and Jerry. She wished that she and Ken could still be playful like that. But it seemed their love life was *over*. The day the doctor confirmed prostate cancer, they knew they were in for some changes. Ken went through a series of tests and then an invasive and painful biopsy that left him, well, impotent. *There's no other word for it.*

During the past several years, he had blood tests and checkups to monitor the development. Surgery was not recommended for several reasons: his age, the small amount of cancer discovered and the fact that the cancer appeared well contained. It was Ken's decision not to go under the knife. So far, his choice had proven to be a good one. Kate was happy with it, too.

Ken and Kate talked often about the impact of Ken's condition on their marriage. One day, they were fine with it; the next, they were sad and depressed. "I don't even remember the last time we made love," Kate muttered, as she pulled into the driveway. "If only I had known it at the time, I could have paid more attention! I could have preserved the memory, to turn to when I feel needy or sad or wanting. It's easy to curl up and throw a pity party. I don't want to do that. It's so self-defeating."

Kate parked the car, took a deep breath and decided to stop whining and just be happy for Colleen and Jerry. They had rediscovered the joy of sex. They had done something for one another—and it was no small thing. "Jerry took a risk," Kate thought aloud. Colleen could have laughed him off. But she responded in just the right away—happily surprised and appreciative. Jerry did something for her, and she did something equally wonderful for him.

Kate walked into the house, set down her jacket and purse and heated a cup of water for tea. *I should do something special for Ken*, she thought. *Something witty, outrageous even!* Kate felt herself growing excited just thinking about it.

Maybe we can't have sex anymore, she thought, *but we can still make love. We have an amazing life, great kids, beautiful grandchildren, good jobs, a lovely home and a God who cares about our every breath! Nothing can get in the way of that—not cancer, not fear, not worry, not self-pity, not regret. Love is so much bigger than the physical act.*

Suddenly Kate jumped to her feet. Even Missy, her cat, stirred at the sound of her shoes hitting the tile. A fabulous idea crossed Kate's mind. "I can't wait to spring this on Ken," she said as she stroked Missy. "But first, I need to call Jerry and Colleen and get some info about where to purchase a certain item!"

I can just see the look on Ken's face, Kate mused with a chuckle, *when I present him with an unexpected gift—a love token that says, "To Ken, from Kate—Good for one 'roll' in the hay. No expiration date!"*

Action

Surprise your spouse (or a dear friend) with a special treat—
something he or she will love but probably won't expect.
Jot down some ideas. Take action on one—or more—of these
ideas!

Reflection

*Dear God, teach me to be spontaneous and generous with everyone
I encounter today—from family and friends to coworkers, even
strangers. A smile, a nod or a word of encouragement may be just
what they need to brighten their day. May I be Your lamp unto
their feet.*

Inspiration

"A good marriage is one which allows for change and growth
in the individuals and in the way they express their love."

—Pearl Buck

Folding Clothes

One of my favorite pastimes during the 1980s was spending a quiet weekend with my husband, Charles, at our little hideaway in Idyllwild, California. We loved to hike in the mountains, rest under shady pine trees, sit on an outcropping of rocks, talk and pray. And one of my least favorite activities was packing up and leaving.

As we wound our way down the mountainside to the freeway and then home to our apartment in San Diego after one of those special weekends, I resisted what lay ahead: piles of dirty laundry to wash, fold and put away; phone calls to return; mail to sort and read; and a calendar reminding me of deadlines and appointments for the coming week. In other words, back to reality!

We pulled into our parking space and unloaded the two duffels stuffed with dirty clothes and hiking boots. Our regularly scheduled wash time in the apartment building where we lived at the time was Thursday morning from 10:00 to noon. However, at times such as this, when we had extra loads, we were expected (house rules!) to fit them in after 10:00 P.M. and before 6:00 A.M.—outside the regular assigned hours.

I was so exhausted from hiking and driving that I could hardly see straight, so I walked right into the laundry room and threw everything into the two washing machines available. Then I went upstairs, cleaned up and fell into bed. I forgot all about switching the clothes from the washers to the dryers—until I sat up straight in the middle of the night and realized what I had done. If I didn't make the switch before morning, I'd mess up the schedule for the entire day. *Oh well,* I told myself, *you can get up at 5:00 and take care of it then.* I fell back to sleep and didn't wake up until 5:45. *Oh no!* I dashed downstairs still in my bathrobe, hoping no one would see me. I was eager to transfer my wet clothes to the dryers before the person who had the 6:00 slot arrived.

Too late! As I pushed open the door, there sat Laverne, my neighbor who lived down the hall. She was leafing through a magazine as the washers and dryers pounded rhythmically beside her.

"Good morning," she said.

"Good morning," I replied. "I'm so sorry . . . last night I got caught up in . . . and I forgot to . . ."

She finished my sentence for me. "Forgot to put your clothes in the dryers?"

"Right," I said as I walked toward the folding tables, too embarrassed to look her in the eye.

I expected to find my wet rumpled clothing in a heap—maybe even with a sign poking out of the soggy mess that read CAN'T YOU FOLLOW HOUSE RULES? Instead I saw several piles of clothing—mine and my husband's—dried and neatly folded, even categorized: socks, shirts, towels, jeans, underwear. All I had to do was stack them in my laundry cart and head upstairs.

"Laverne, did you . . ." I gestured to the clothing.

"I did," she said, smiling. "I got here early today, so why not?"

"I feel bad that you had to mess with our clothes at all. But then you dried and folded them too! What an angel you are."

Laverne looked at me, her bright eyes brimming with kindness. "I didn't mind," she said. "Isn't that what we're here for? To help each other?"

Slowly, I rolled her words over in my mind. *Isn't that what we're here for? To help each other?*

Here was a woman who knew how to love a neighbor. She sure taught me a thing or two that morning. More important, she demonstrated it. And it didn't have anything to do with folding clothes. I hugged her tight, piled my laundry into my basket and went upstairs—feeling better than I had in weeks.

Fortunately for me, Laverne didn't abide by the rules of the "me first" part of our culture: Don't do for others what they can do for themselves. In fact, I doubt she even knew that doing for others had earned a bad reputation—that it could be construed as codependent behavior or, worse yet, as a way to avoid looking at one's own life. No, Laverne didn't do any of that. She just did what came naturally to her. She helped a neighbor, a friend in need.

I took her lead, and in turn, I did something for someone else that day. How could I not? *Isn't that what we're here for?* I reminded myself.

Action

Consider what you might do today to surprise someone with an unexpected gift from your heart. Perhaps it will surprise you, too!

Reflection

Lord, God, I want to be like Laverne. Help me to be more conscious of the needs of those around me and less focused on my own.

Inspiration

"The good neighbor looks beyond the external accidents and discerns those inner qualities that make all men human and, therefore, brothers."

—Martin Luther King, Jr.

Invisible Gifts

Chloe pulled a large box from the cabinet in the den and reached inside for glittery wrapping paper and a large silver bow. "Elizabeth's going to love this," she said turning to Poochie. "Don't you think? Every teenaged daughter looks forward to a special present from her mom. What better gift than a cashmere sweater—and it matches her blue eyes."

The dog barked and then lay at her feet. "You need a snuggle, don't you, sweet one?"

Chloe patted Poochie and scratched the dog's neck. Poochie wagged her tail and sat perfectly still. "You don't ask for much, do you?" she said. "Just a good meal, a warm place to sleep and some cuddling. I guess we could all use more of that. And time to be together. What a gift that is."

Chloe walked into the kitchen and poured a cup of coffee. She mulled over what she had just said. *Time. What a gift!*

Suddenly an idea struck her. *Why hadn't I thought of this sooner?* she said to herself. She set aside the sweater and took a piece of stationery from her desk. She knew exactly what Elizabeth wanted. A sweater was probably the last item on her list. Her daughter had been telling her for weeks—sometimes openly and sometimes subtly—what she really wanted. She wanted time with her mother, time to bake cookies, to snuggle on the sofa together and watch a video, to walk on the beach, to shop and to talk with no interruptions.

But Chloe had been preoccupied with her real estate business, the endless meetings and her worries about bringing in enough money for the two of them. She glanced at the photo of her husband, Ted, on the wall above her desk. "We need you," she said as her eyes filled up. "God, why? I don't get it. Ted is with You, and You seem far away. I can't do this alone. I'm scared. And I see fear in Elizabeth's eyes, too."

Then Chloe remembered something her grandmother often told her as a kid: "The Lord is a strong tower. Run to Him whenever you're afraid." She knew in her heart that He would never leave her nor forsake her. He had promised! It was up to her to receive His promise and to live in it.

Chloe focused on the stationery in front of her. She plucked the kitchen scissors from a drawer and cut the paper into several rectangles. Then she began writing. When she finished, she had 12 gift coupons for Elizabeth— one for each month of the year.

January: *Good for lunch with me—you pick the place.*

February: *Good for one afternoon of shopping—your choice of mall.*

March: *Good for a back rub—you name the time!*

And on she went.

The best one she saved for April, Elizabeth's birthday month: *Good for one invisible gift—see if you recognize it.*

Chloe smiled as she wrote that one. She knew that a smile, a kind word, a listening ear, an apology when she was wrong, the disavowal of her right to be right when they had a disagreement might be among the best gifts of all. These gifts would bless her daughter in a way that a gift in a box never could. She knew that her presence meant so much more to Elizabeth than a mere present—just as God's presence in her life meant more than anything else.

Chloe decorated each gift certificate with a colorful sticker, clipped them together and placed them in the box. She laid the sweater on top. She couldn't wait for Elizabeth to come home. Things were going to be different—in the best of ways. She studied the image of her husband once more. "We're going to be all right," she said.

Action
Create a book of coupons for someone special in your life—a friend, a daughter or son, a parent or your spouse. Jot down a list of activities and items that are especially pleasing to that person and then get started!

Reflection
Lord, Jesus, how quick I am to overlook the real needs of those I love. I'm so focused on what I think they should want or need that I miss out entirely. Help me today to stop, look and listen and then to act in a way that nurtures and blesses.

Inspiration
"The best inheritance a parent can give his children is a few minutes of his time each day."

—O. A. Battista

*MY INTERCESSOR IS MY FRIEND AS MY EYES
POUR OUT TEARS TO GOD.*

JOB 16:20

Howdy, Heartner!

My friend and writing colleague Lynni and I have decided to be "heartners" (our code word for "partners of the heart"). Can't you just see us strumming our gee-tars and tipping our Western hats to a crowd of onlookers? Not exactly! We both sing, but that's where the similarity to those wearing fringe jackets and pointy-toed boots ends.

So what does the term "heartner" mean to us? It means we support one another at work, at home and in our community with ongoing prayer, a listening ear or two, a heart of love, lots of e-mail chats, advice when solicited and silence when it's not, and accountability—a fancy word for the freedom to say at times, "You did *what?*"

Sometimes being a heart partner can take you to the edge. One more step and the relationship will go over the cliff. You're sure of it. But still, you *have* to take the step—you have to be willing to risk—or you're no partner and certainly not a heartner. You're an accomplice!

I remember a time when I spoke my heart (and mind) to a friend about a decision she had made to marry a man I didn't trust. In fact, I felt like putting a detective on his trail for a few weeks. But my friend was in love. She defended her choice. She stood by her man! She married him. And she stopped speaking to me—for a time. Today she's divorced. Today we're friends again.

I also recall a time when a woman spoke truth in my ear. She showed me that my grumbling was pulling me down and affecting my work, my family and my relationships. "You have a lot to be grateful for," she reminded me. "Start paying attention to the *gifts*, and give thanks."

I listened—reluctantly at first but then willingly. And my life changed from one of "If only . . ." to "Thank You, Lord, for this new day and all it holds for me."

You might want to find a heartner in your life—a friend who will support you in the workplace as well as at home, who will keep a mind and heart open to your needs and desires, and who will hold you fast to the high road with prayer and honest questions when you're about to stray. We all need individuals in our lives who *care* enough to *be there* in the trivial, in the trials *and* in the triumphs, too.

J. I. Packer, in a chapter on prayer in his book *Knowing Christianity*, reminds us that we should not forget "the special benefit of praying with a like-minded Christian who is committed both to God and to you . . . happy then is the one who finds such a partner, and stupid is the person who never seeks one. . . . It is good when we can travel two by two."[1]

Happy trails!

Action

List the names of your close women friends. Beside each name, jot down something special about that woman. Pray over each one and ask God to indicate which one would be a suitable heartner for you. When you receive your answer, call that woman and invite her to tea or for a walk and ask her whether she'd like to join with you in prayer and support. You will not regret it.

Reflection

God, I like the idea of finding a woman to partner with in prayer. Please help me find just the right one so that we will be a blessing to one another.

Inspiration

"Women give nothing to friendship except what they borrow from love."

—Chamfort

Note

1. J. I. Packer, *Knowing Christianity* (Downers Grove, IL: InterVarsity Press, 1999), pp. 132-133.

Tea and Thee

I waved good-bye and threw last-minute kisses to my children and husband as they left for school and work. It was the first week of what I hoped would be the rest of my life in our beautiful new home in Calabasas, California. I walked into the kitchen from the driveway, looked around, and then suddenly burst into tears.

What is the matter with me? I wondered. *This is my dream house.* We had planned every detail of our move for months. We knew it was God's gift to us. This home offered more room for our growing family of five, a lovely yard overlooking a wild canyon, a huge kitchen with all the modern conveniences and the perfect place outdoors to create a rose bed.

As I sat at the kitchen table that morning, however, nothing mattered. I was in grief. I missed the old house, the comfortable neighborhood, the familiar church and school and all the people I had come to know and love during the previous eight years. The kids had been able to walk to school and I could run our dog to the park, just two blocks away. I wondered if I'd ever feel at home in this big house, on this block where I didn't know another soul.

I poked at the scrambled eggs that had grown cold and stared out the window. Even the blue sky and the giant oaks on the hillside could not take my mind off the remorse I felt. I wondered whether we had made a terrible mistake.

"Lord, help me get a grip," I prayed.

I stacked the dishes in the sink, splashed cold water on my face and trudged upstairs to my study. I did my best to console myself. *Maybe if I unpack some boxes and put things in order I'll feel more at home,* I thought.

I pulled out the step stool, climbed to the top and heaved a bunch of books into the bookcase. Then I placed some family photos here and there on lower shelves. I hung a few paintings and . . . hey, the place was starting to *feel* like me! Then suddenly I heard the front doorbell ring. I looked out and saw a woman about my age standing on the landing.

"Oh, great," I mumbled. "Someone wants to sell me something. Well, I'm not buying!" I dabbed my eyes with a tissue, tucked my shirt into my jeans and jogged down the stairs.

"Hello," said the woman when I opened the door. "I'm Jean Sanchez. I live in the yellow house at the end of the cul-de-sac. Welcome to our neighborhood."

She extended her hand and I accepted it. Her smile could win over anyone!

"I would have come sooner," she added, "but I wanted to give you a few days to get settled." Then she handed me a lovely glass jar with a blue bow on top.

"I call this concoction friendship tea," she said, chuckling. "It's a mixture of iced tea crystals and an orange drink mix. Add water, stir, toss in a few cubes of ice and enjoy! The recipe is right here," she said, pointing to the card she had taped to the bottom of the jar. "And here are a dozen lemon crisps to go with it."

I was overwhelmed. I had been quick to assume the worst about her. And now here she was offering me a gift of friendship and welcoming me to the neighborhood.

Tears welled in my eyes again—but this time, not from grief, but from gratitude. Here was a gift so lovely, so unexpected, so like the Lord that I was speechless—pretty unusual for me!

I reached out and hugged Jean, thanked her and then invited this new friend in to share a cup of friendship tea with me.

Action

Who would enjoy a cup of friendship tea with you? Consider a neighbor, an elderly person who may be alone, a young girl, a teenaged friend, a new acquaintance. How lovely it would be to brew a pot and then invite her over to sip and chat.

Reflection

Lord, God, what a sweet experience it is to enjoy conversation with a friend over a cup of tea. Thank You for the gift of new friends and old, the silver and gold of life.

Inspiration

"Small cheer and great welcome makes a merry feast."

—William Shakespeare

THOUGH ONE MAY BE OVERPOWERED, TWO CAN
DEFEND THEMSELVES. A CORD OF THREE STRANDS
IS NOT QUICKLY BROKEN.

ECCLESIASTES 4:12

Rings and Things

"Mom, I'd like to have that ring after you . . . well . . . you know . . . after you're gone," my adult daughter commented one day—with a guilty smile. "I'm not in a rush," she added, backpedaling her words fast. "Will you save it for me?"

I was glad to hear she wasn't in a hurry to get rid of me. I was also pleased she liked the diamond and moonstone ring that my father had given me enough to want to inherit it one day. When my daughter receives it, it truly will be an heirloom.

I learned about heirloom jewelry from Mark Beauchamp, owner of Jewelry by Design in San Diego, California. Mark specializes in designing pieces that will likely become heirlooms. "Generally, a piece of jewelry becomes an heirloom when it is passed down to the second generation," he told me. "It's not always planned, but it can be, and when it is, the piece is even more meaningful."

A ring or a pin or a bracelet becomes a symbol of what is meaningful to you. "Custom-designed engagement and wedding rings, for example," says Mark, "are tangible inheritances that endure long after the life of the bride and groom, reminding present and future family members of the couple's contribution to the family. Heirlooms deepen the meaning of a special occasion because they are set apart from ordinary pieces bought off the shelf."

I have a custom-made gold ring that includes my and my children's birthstones and the gold from my wedding and engagement rings from their father—even though he and I are divorced. I see the ring as a precious symbol of our family and what we still have, even though our life today has a different form from the one it had when we were all together.

My husband, Charles, and I personalized our wedding rings, which we hope one day our children and grandchildren will cherish. We took the diamond from an heirloom ring that my husband had received from his father and had it placed in the center of a ring designed especially for Charles. The jeweler then created my ring to complement his. Whenever I look at our rings, I am reminded that we are equally yoked under Christ.

Some Christians believe it is wrong to put our attention on things of this world. "The problem with this viewpoint," claims Mark, "is that the next generation is neglected. It does not consider the importance of caring for one's children and grandchildren by passing on tangible gifts that reflect one's values and one's faith. I believe we have a mandate to leave a heritage and an inheritance for our children and their children."

Thoughtful, custom-designed rings and other pieces of jewelry for special occasions are gifts in the present, a testimony to the heritage of your past and a blessing to pass on to future generations. These sacred symbols will remind future generations of your commitment to Christ and to your family.

Action

Is there a piece of jewelry you'd like to have made or is there one you already have that you'd like to pass on to a child or a grandchild? Begin planning now.

Reflection

Lord, You are my treasure. May I pass on to others my love for You by the actions I take, the prayers I pray and the gifts I share, both tangible and intangible.

Inspiration

"I rejoice in life for its own sake. Life is no brief candle to me; it is a sort of splendid torch which I've got a hold of for the moment and I want to make it burn as brightly as possible before handing it on to future generations."

—George Bernard Shaw

Precept 2

Do Something for Yourself

DO NOT BE WISE IN YOUR OWN EYES; FEAR THE LORD
AND SHUN EVIL. THIS WILL BRING HEALTH TO YOUR
BODY AND NOURISHMENT TO YOUR BONES.
PROVERBS 3:7-8

Now *there's* a concept—doing something for yourself—but what and when? If you find the time, what might you do? Perhaps your mind is as blank as a fresh sheet of paper. You've daydreamed about flying an airplane, singing in front of 5,000 people, writing a novel, going back to college, starting your own business. But those goals are big and far-off. You'd be happy with something small, something really doable at this stage of your life, but you can't think of anything right off the top of your head.

Those ideas will come forward when you rid yourself of the clutter that is weighing them down. At least that was true for me. I kept pushing my desires aside, even the fairly simple ones, such as getting a professional massage, taking needlepoint lessons or going on a bike ride alone. Instead of listening to myself, I listened to everyone else, and I followed their dreams instead of mine—until one day I got the message that I could start small and I could start *now*.

The stories in this section will encourage you to do something for yourself *now*. You'll read about a mother bird and the lesson she unwittingly taught another mother without saying a word! A woman realizes she is quick to support a friend in living her dream but has neglected her own. The wilderness is a place of challenge and self-discovery for one woman during a hike to Half Dome in Yosemite. Sometimes saying no is the best thing we can do for ourselves, as one woman comes to understand. Nature helps a woman to see her own beauty—at last—and give herself the acknowledgment she deserves! And finally, a grandmother and her grandson discover journal writing as a way to do something for themselves.

Room with a View

"Look, Charles," I called from the front deck. "We have company!"

"Hold 'em off," Charles shouted from the bathroom. "I'm not dressed yet."

"Not a problem for these folks. They run around in their birthday suits all the time!"

"Very funny," he said as he wrapped himself in a towel and met me at the doorway. "Who are you referring to? I didn't hear anyone knock."

"A bird—a mourning dove," I said, pointing to the delicate creature perched in the ficus tree in the corner. "Looks like Mama Bird is setting up housekeeping. I wonder if she'll have twins or maybe triplets. Isn't this exciting?"

"It'll be cute for a day or two," he said, "but you'll see. There will be droppings everywhere! Are you volunteering to clean up after her?"

I hadn't thought about that. But now that he mentioned it, I said, "Okay." How often does a person get to watch a mother bird build a nest, scrap by scrap, string by string, twig by twig, and then lay her eggs and keep them warm till they hatch?

This bird was pretty savvy! She knew her real estate. She had picked the tree on our deck overlooking beautiful San Diego Bay—definitely a room with a view.

For the next several weeks, Charles and I woke up every morning eager to see what Mama was up to next. Soon a second bird appeared in the tree. Papa, perhaps? It appeared so, and after Mama laid her eggs, the two birds exchanged places every hour or so round the clock as near as I could tell. He took a break while she nestled the eggs. Then she "took five" while he snuggled them. The changing of the guard was a precious sight. Not for a moment were the eggs exposed to the air. Papa flew in, gently nudged Mama, and she then slid off to one side as he moved into place. The same thing occurred when she returned from her break. They also kept in touch when they were apart. I heard one or the other "mourning" softly, "coo, coo," just before returning.

Mama also had her priorities in the right place. She focused on her task—keeping the eggs warm. She wasn't into housekeeping. In fact, I wondered at times if the nest would make it. A twig here, a leaf there spilled out the sides, but she didn't stop for repairs. She stayed with her young.

I couldn't help but think of the times I put housecleaning in front of spending time with my kids! *Oh, Mama Bird, I thought, you are here for a purpose beyond hatching your young. I'm going to watch you. You have much to teach me.*

And teach me she did! I stayed with her throughout the gestation period and through the growth of her hatchlings. I watched the hatchlings leave the nest, walk around our deck, flap their delicate wings, and then one day take off into the world for whatever God had planned for them.

This experience reminded me of words I saw on a plaque that hung in my parents' bedroom: "There are only two lasting things we can give our children. One is roots; the other, wings."

By God's grace, I would do the same. Mother birds and human mothers have more in common than I ever would have imagined!

Action

What are your priorities? Make a list, and don't forget to include something for yourself. When you reserve time and energy for your desires and needs, you'll have plenty of time and enthusiasm left to support others.

Reflection

Lord, lately I haven't thought much about setting priorities. They seem to set themselves, and I follow without resistance. It's time to change that wishy-washy way of living. Please help me today to determine what's important and necessary and lovely and then help me make it happen in the order You establish.

Inspiration

"I believe one of the most important priorities is to do whatever we do as well as we can. We should take pride in that."

—Victor Kiam

Coming Clean

"Nance, I want to go back to school and finish my degree and become a teacher," Nance's friend Marissa blurted in one great breath. She began shredding the paper napkin in her hand as the two friends sat on a park bench and sipped coffee after their morning walk.

"There. I've said it. I've finally come clean," she rushed on. "I've been dying to tell you, but it seems so far-off and so *big*. Do you think I can do it?"

Nance looked at this woman who had been her best friend since high school and didn't know what to say. She never knew Marissa wanted to do anything other than be a wife and mom and work part-time as a grocery clerk. Marissa hated change.

Nance grabbed her hand and squeezed it. "Mar, what a wonderful goal. I'm so glad you let it out. What can I do to support you?"

"Stick with me. Nance, I worry that it's too late. I'm 45 now, and by the time I finish course work and then student teach, I'll be 50!" She scowled at the thought of hitting the big 5-0!

"In five years you'll be 50 anyway," Nance joked. "But you'll be a 50-year-old teacher instead of a 50-year-old woman who regrets not taking charge of her life. How does that sound?"

Marissa burst out laughing. "I never thought of it *that* way. Nance, you're such an encourager. I should have known I could trust you with this. Maybe it's me I can't trust. Now that it's out in the open, it feels so scary. I'm not sure where to start."

"You've already started," Nance said. "You put it into words. God knows your heart. He'll show you the way."

They walked to their cars, hugged good-bye and agreed to meet the following Monday— same time, same spot.

Nance drove home thinking about Marissa and her dream. *Did I have a dream of my own?* she wondered. Nance mulled the thought for the rest of the day. She had been working as a nurse in pediatrics for 20 years. She was happy in her job, but lately she felt restless. She needed something creative in her life. She thought, *I'm willing to support Marissa doing something for herself, but am I willing to do something for myself?*

During the next few days, Nance thought about what *she'd* like to do and prayed for direction. On Friday, she got up the courage to open an old trunk she had put into the garage years before. Her hands shook as she popped the lid and saw the art supplies she had carefully packed away: easel, brushes, a canvas with a sketch half-finished. Nance sat down and wept. *Why had I abandoned my goal of painting? So many people had encouraged me when I was in school. But I didn't believe I could make it. How would I pay my bills?* She gave herself a good talking to! She shoved the desire and the dream into a battered trunk and slammed the lid on both.

Now here she was at age 50, overcome with sadness for what could have been—maybe even what would have been— if she hadn't listened to her own critical voice. *Do something useful with your life. Think of others, not yourself. Nurses help people. What do artists do? Sit around putting paint on canvas. How useful is that?*

Then a small memory jogged to the edge of Nance's mind: her mother sitting at an easel in the backyard. Nance must have been six or seven at the time. Nance loved watching her mother paint. Her mother's long blond hair sparkled in the sun, and she smiled as she dabbed her brush into the palette of colors and then stroked the canvas until it came alive with a flower or a tree or a little brook. Nance wanted to do that. She wanted to put the pictures in her mind on canvas and show them to the world. "Look! I'm a painter!" she wanted to shout. But she never did.

When Nance's dad went off to the Vietnam War, her mother put away her paints and easel. Nance never saw her take them out again. Nance's dream went into the attic with her mother's. She dabbled at painting while in high school, but then enrolled in nursing school—and that was the end of that.

Tears gushed down Nance's cheeks and onto her shirt. She pulled out a tissue and blew her nose. She hadn't cried like this in a long time. She realized she hadn't smiled with her heart in a long time either.

"Mom," Nance called to the heavens, "I'm taking up painting again, for you and for me. What do you think of that?"

Nance could almost see her mother's blond hair sparkling in the sun and her hand reaching for Nance's. Nance knew this is exactly what her mother would want her to do. And she knew that God wanted it for her, too.

Action

What do you *really* want to do? What thought has nudged you—perhaps for years? Take some time to consider your talents and gifts. How do you want to use them in the world for good? Consider what step you can take today to get started, and then take it.

Reflection

Lord, You have given me talent, intelligence and opportunity, but I've held back from using them, out of fear, uncertainty and lack of confidence. Please help me today to put aside these human concerns and to put my hand in Yours as You lead me to use my gifts in a way that will glorify You and bless me.

Inspiration

"In absence of clearly defined goals, we become strangely loyal to performing daily acts of trivia."

—Anonymous

On the Wild Side

I slipped into the soft warmth of my down sleeping bag. Stars dotted the blackness above. Wind blew through the tall pines and rustled my tent. I breathed deeply. Relief swept through me. It was the last night of a week in the wilderness with 14 other "mountain mamas" from age 33 to 76. And what a week it had been. Everyone had made it to the 10,000-feet elevation where we settled in for a week beside Davis Lake in the Sierra Mountains in Northern California. It was our annual All-Gals Mule Pack trip.

Mules had hauled our heavy gear—60 pounds per person that first day. We carried in our backpacks whatever else we wanted—extras such as a favorite book, a special hat, snacks, water and, of course, rain gear and first-aid items—for the five-hour hike to our destination.

As we hiked up, up and up—nearly 3,000 feet in all—trees, tall and sturdy against the blue sky, called out to be hugged. Mountains guarded sprawling meadows, home to a profusion of flowers in full color: lupine, columbine, Indian paintbrush, baby blue eyes, shooting stars, monkey flowers and mule's ears. And snowmelt spilled down mountainsides in cascading waterfalls.

Each day thereafter we hiked to a different spot—a far-off lake, a tall peak, a high meadow. But it took some grit to get there. We scrambled over boulders, plodded through snow fields (stopping long enough for a midsummer snow-ball fight!) and walked across rushing streams. Our hearts pounded, blood coursed through our veins, the sun beat down, and mosquitoes nibbled whatever bit of skin we hadn't covered.

We would come "home" each night, strip off our damp and dusty clothing, pull on swimsuits and head for the beach—yes, a sandy beach just steps from our campsite—for a quick dip in the ice-cold lake. Brrr! But so refreshing.

As the sun set, we pulled on comfy fleece pants and jackets, caps and gloves and shared hot soups and stews, crackers, cookies, candy, soothing tea and fresh-brewed coffee. Then we settled down for a sing-along, a story time and games around the campfire before a long and much-needed sleep.

A bear wandered among our tents the first and second nights, but he didn't find enough to hold his interest. We had locked up our food in bear-proof canisters, so off he went in search of something better. Whew!

I led a journal-writing session each afternoon. It was a special time for us to pause, reflect, write, share and give thanks for God's gifts we'd been privileged to witness and receive.

Cool water from a rushing stream quenched our thirst, revived our spirits as well as our parched skin and, when boiled, turned dry food packets into delicious meals.

Fire under our miniature stoves heated our food, warmed our hands and comforted our souls on a chilly evening. And the stars and moon put on a bountiful show each night.

I realized once again why I come to the Sierra year after year after year, why I come to this wild place and why I want everyone to know about its beauty and wonder. It is here that one gets to see what really matters. A new outfit doesn't matter, nor does the latest automobile, cruise tickets or dinner at a five-star restaurant.

What we needed we (and the mules) carried. What we couldn't carry, God, through nature, provided. A cluster of boulders and rocks and a few sturdy tree limbs were the only furniture required. A bed of pine needles made a comfortable carpet for our tents. A broad old tree offered a fallen branch for a seat, limbs for hanging wet socks and foliage for shade.

Hours and hours of time to be still in the silence gives one an entirely new perspective on life, both in the mountains where the wild things grow and in the city where we're too much on the go! It is here that I am able to be still—and know that *God is God*. It is here that I am able to go out in joy and be led forth in peace, as the Scripture promises. And all around me the mountains and the hills burst into song before their creator, and "the trees of the field clap their hands" (Isa. 55:12).

On the final day, I looked around once again, swiped at the tears rolling down my face and whispered to the heavens, "Thank you for this wild place where wild things grow and where *I* grow in grace and gratitude."

Action

Set a date with a friend or family member (or even with yourself alone) to get out into nature, whether a walk along a stream or river, a stroll in the woods or a hike in the mountains. Experience the beauty around you. Drink up the sunshine, smell the flowers, hug a tree! You may be surprised at what a difference it will make in your body and in your spirit.

Reflection

Dear Lord, today I thank You for the gift of Your creation, the fruit on the vine, the flowers in bloom, the wind in my hair, the scent of the pine trees.

Inspiration

"Climb the mountains and get their good tidings. Nature's peace will flow into you as sunshine flows into trees. The winds will blow their own freshness into you, and the storms their energy, while cares will drop away from you like the leaves of autumn."

—John Muir

Kitchen Angel

It was Sunday morning, and my husband and I had arrived early for worship service. While Charles chatted with a friend, I leafed through the church bulletin. The headline "Wanted: Kitchen Angels" caught my attention. *What's this about?* I wondered. I read on. Rita, one of the ladies in our congregation, was forming a committee of men and women who were willing to prepare and deliver meals to those in need, such as new mothers, those who were sick or housebound, and so on. The notice made it clear that if enough people signed up, the burden would be spread out to such a degree that no one would be overwhelmed. A one-meal-a-month commitment was all that was required.

I pulled out my pen and signed up on the spot. *I can do this!* I cheered internally. What an easy way to contribute to our church family. And it was a great thing to do for myself, as well, because I love to cook.

Now I no longer need to feel guilty about not going on a short-term missions trip or building homes for the homeless in Mexico, I reasoned, *or teaching Sunday School lessons to five-year-olds.*

When the first call came in, I was ready to serve! I darned near saluted and clicked my heels as I said yes to the assignment. A young woman had just given birth to twins. Her husband worked irregular hours in law enforcement, and her mother, though helpful with the babies, couldn't be expected to cook wholesome meals, too! So a group of us were enlisted to take turns providing a nourishing dinner each evening for the next two weeks.

When it was my turn, I outdid myself. I prepared Italian chicken and mushrooms with all the trimmings: green salad with candied pecans, garlic-stuffed olives, cherry tomatoes and baby carrots laced with a homemade vinaigrette dressing. I prepared a savory garlic-butter mixture to spread on crunchy Italian bread and made chocolate cake for dessert with fancy frosting and the words "Welcome Home" across the top. I put the ingredients into two beautiful baskets with a bottle of Chianti for the wine drinkers and a bottle of grape juice for the others. I brought my own dishes and tableware so that the grandmother would not have to lift a finger!

The meal and the service were a hit. The family thanked me profusely, and I went home flying. I had found my calling. I was truly a kitchen angel.

The next month I had a new assignment. I was rushed when the call came in, so I put together a grocery market dinner for that family: barbecued chicken and pasta salad from the deli, a pie and a loaf of bread from the bakery. They were on their own for drinks and dishes. I brought the meal in two large shopping bags. I had just enough time to drop off the food and say, "Have a nice evening."

These assignments continued for more than a year. Sometimes I'd turn down an opportunity because I couldn't fit it into my already-packed schedule, and sometimes I simply didn't *want* to say yes because it meant driving across town in rush-hour traffic! I was growing resentful; then I felt guilty about feeling that way. My wings were drooping. I was anything but a kitchen angel.

The Lord broke through to me, however, when I broke down on the phone with Rita, who called to offer me another opportunity. I told her I just couldn't keep up with the demand, even though it was rarely more than once a month, as promised. I found myself saying no more than yes and making lame excuses, as well as avoiding eye contact with other kitchen angels at church. I was certain my reputation preceded me, and the word was out: Karen was a fallen angel!

"Would you like to retire (read *resign*) from Kitchen Angels?" Rita asked when I hemmed and hawed in response to her request.

"Oh no. I mean this is a wonderful ministry, and I love being part of it," I lied. Actually, it is a wonderful ministry, just not wonderful for me any longer. The truth is that after the first couple of assignments, I hated being a kitchen angel. I don't mind cooking for my husband and myself and for company or visiting family, but I'm not the catering type. I generally decide what to have for dinner about 20 minutes before we eat. I don't like cookbooks, and I'm not into elaborate planning, except for very special occasions—such as a presidential or papal visit!

Rita pressed me—gently. "It's okay, Karen," she said. "No shame in letting go of something that no longer works for you—that no longer brings you *joy.*" There was that word again. "We've appreciated having you on the team for as long as you've been able. What do you say?"

"I agree," I muttered, trying to hold myself together. I felt like a failure. I envisioned men and women and little children who couldn't get out, who couldn't cook for themselves, who needed someone like me to help, at least temporarily. But I knew I could not pretend any longer. I was not serving them or myself. I was trying to turn a lie into a truth—and it wasn't working. So I did the church a favor, the team a favor and, most of all, myself a favor. I retired and turned in my wings!

Since then, I've been telling the truth as soon as I know it—about what I really want to do *for myself.* I want to sing (so I'm now in the choir). I want to speak (so I lead retreats and other women's events). I want to hike and camp (so I spend at least one week a year in the Sierra Mountains and one or more days a month hiking in the hills near my home).

It has taken a while, but now I understand that when I do something really good for myself, I'm doing something really good for others at the same time.

Action

What are you now doing that you no longer feel excited about or interested in—or are even worn out with? Perhaps you're chair of a committee that you don't enjoy. Perhaps you signed up to bake cookies for a dessert buffet and you hate to bake! Or perhaps you've lassoed yourself into learning how to quilt because your friend said it would be fun, but now you dread the classes. Maybe it's time to rethink what you do and don't want to do, and then take action. Decide today, so there will be time and space in your life to take on what you love and care about. After all, God is the One who put those dreams and desires in your heart.

Reflection

Lord, God, help me choose one thing that would honor You, and then make me happy to do it instead of merely thinking about it. Help me discover Your plan, and then please give me the grace to make it a reality.

Inspiration

"We can't take any credit for our talents. It's how we use them that counts."

—Madeleine L'Engle

Humps and Bumps

"Charles, look, there's the turnoff for the White Mountains."
I pointed to the sign on the road that led from Highway 395
in Big Pine, California, up to the ancient Bristlecone Pines.
"Let's add a day on our way back from camping and make
the trip. This is something I've wanted to do for years."

"Okay, I'm game," he said.

A week later, after our camping trip in Mammoth,
California, we drove the winding road and parked in front
of the ranger station. The air was thin and chilly at 12,000
feet. We grabbed our parkas and hats and panted our way
up to the front door.

Minutes later we had a map in hand and set out to walk
the four-mile trail that led through a forest of ancient
pines—some nearly 5,000 years old. One tree in particular,
dubbed "Methuselah," was the oldest of all. Its location is
kept secret, so it won't be abused. We had fun guessing
which one it might be.

We returned to our car and decided then to make the
12-mile ride to the Patriarch Forest where there was another
trail through a grove of ancient trees, many among the oldest in the world. The unpaved road was bumpy and strewn
with rocks; the air was hot and thick with dust. I felt like a

pioneer in a covered wagon! We had a mission to accomplish, and we weren't going to stop until we met our goal. The further we drove, however, the more anxious I became. It seemed we'd never arrive. The afternoon sun was already tilting to the west, and I feared we wouldn't make it back before it set. At the same time, I also felt exhilarated by the adventure into the unknown. We pressed on and finally saw a small sign that led to a parking lot beside the grove.

I jumped out of the car, eager to hug a tree. The silence was profound. We'd made it! We walked the trail, stopping here and there to comment on the shape or color or texture of these amazing specimens that were the only survivors in this soil for thousands of years. I could hardly put my mind around this fact. I felt a kind of reverence for each tree. I wanted to congratulate them for making it, for being steadfast, for doing what God had created them to do. They had survived this barren place yet were still standing, proof of the stuff they were made of.

Knots, humps, bumps, gnarled branches and chubby trunks abounded. These trees were not beautiful like a graceful willow or tall and slender like a stately palm, but they were elegant in their own way. The ravages of age and weather had given them a beauty impossible to describe.

Then I thought about myself, an older woman who had a few humps and bumps of my own. I had been discounting myself lately, finding fault with the changes my body reflected and with the aging process that had become more evident each year. In a flash of insight, I suddenly wept. *How is it that I could see beauty in the trees but not in myself? Why is getting older a good thing for a tree, but a bad thing for me? Why do I look in the mirror and bemoan the wrinkles that line my face but see in the trees a quiet dignity that has nothing to do with shape or age?*

Charles and I drove back in silence, each of us wrapped in thought. What had begun as a pleasant side trip turned into a personal retreat. Bubbling conversation had given way to quiet reflection.

Oh Lord, I prayed, *how ungrateful of me to judge my worth by how I look. I know that I am more to You than a lump of aging clay. Thank You for the gifts of wisdom and discernment, for curiosity, for peace, and for Your everlasting love.*

Action

Do you spend time analyzing and criticizing yourself? Are you envious of other women who may have the curly hair or expressive hands, eye color or body shape you wish were yours? Today, set aside those life-depleting thoughts and turn your mind to what is lovely and pretty and health-giving about yourself at this stage of your life. Make a list, if necessary, and then tell God in prayer how grateful you are to be *you!*

Reflection

Dear Lord, help me to focus on what You've blessed me with, not on the attributes and traits You've given to someone else. I want to be a woman of gratitude rather than one who judges and compares.

Inspiration

"There is no excellent beauty that hath not some strangeness in the proportion."

—Sir Francis Bacon

WRITE DOWN THE REVELATION AND MAKE IT PLAIN ON TABLETS.

HABAKKUK 2:2

Dear Journal

"Isn't this fun, Magah (the name my first grandson dubbed me when he learned to talk)? Just the two of us?" Eight-year-old Noah hopped out of the car and onto a nearby rock and then onto a log and then onto a picnic table and then onto another rock. The fun had begun. It was Friday afternoon. We had just arrived at Foster Lodge in the Laguna Mountains, east of San Diego, California, for the annual Sierra Club's Nature Knowledge Workshop, a weekend for adults and children devoted to the study of nature. I was as excited about being with my grandson as he was about being with me.

We hurried into the rustic lodge, staked out a comfortable bunk bed, stashed our backpacks and duffel bags and then joined the other moms, dads, grandparents and children who were gathering in the main room. We signed up for the workshops and hikes that most appealed to us, among them: Hike to the Boulders, Nature Art, Insect Study, Botany Walk. We also signed up for our turn to serve food and clear the dining room tables after meals.

Perhaps the most significant element of the weekend was journal writing. Noah wanted to take home some tangible memories of the weekend to add to his interest in science and to share with his family. I wanted to jot down what happened for me on our grandmother-grandson weekend.

Noah unpacked his journal first thing and made sure he had it with us at all times. I took mental notes of my experiences and impressions and jotted them down when I had a quiet moment on my own.

As soon as we completed a hike or a walk or a lecture, Noah pulled out his journal, handed it to me, and then dictated three or four sentences that summarized his experience. I wrote down exactly what he said. He was an excellent reader but was still mastering his writing skills, so it helped him to have me there to get his thoughts down before they got away.

After viewing a slide show on animal behavior, he wrote: "The snake ate a whole squirrel and it took thirty minutes to finish it. If you see a mountain lion, don't run. Make yourself look big by putting your arms over your head and pushing out your muscles." Following a lecture on conservation, he dictated the following: "I learned a new word. Biodegradable. It means things used from nature go back into the earth." I helped him put those new concepts on paper.

I had a few observations of my own—truly a gift to myself that I will reread and enjoy during the years to come—the pleasure of time spent with my dear grandson, the beauty of nature everywhere we looked, the soft night sounds around us as we cuddled in our sleeping cocoons and the hand-in-hand walks we shared in the cool morning hours, after skipping over rocks and jumping over logs!

Sunday afternoon we said good-bye to the new friends we had made and the adult leaders who had made the trip possible. Then we packed my car and took off. A couple of hours later, we met Noah's father in our usual meeting place, and the first words out of Noah's mouth were, "Dad, Dad, want to hear my journal?"

I had captured most of our experiences on film, so the following week I sent Noah a small photo album of pictures with captions—a gift of love and memories. We had shared a very special time together as grandmother and grandson, and we had also learned more about God's green earth and the bounty of natural gifts He has provided. And because of Noah's journal—and mine—we have it not only in our hearts and minds but on paper as well, for all time.

Action

Start keeping a journal or diary for yourself, your children or your grandchildren. Jot down the things you want to remember, the feelings you experience and the details you wish to hold on to. Add to it whenever you like. There is no one way to do this. Let the Spirit lead you. What a lovely gift to yourself and to those who will receive it after you're gone.

Reflection

Dear Lord, one thing of great value I can do for myself is to keep a written record of memorable events and experiences in my life. Help me to start such a project and to remain committed to it.

Inspiration

"Journal writing is a voyage to the interior."

—Christina Baldwin

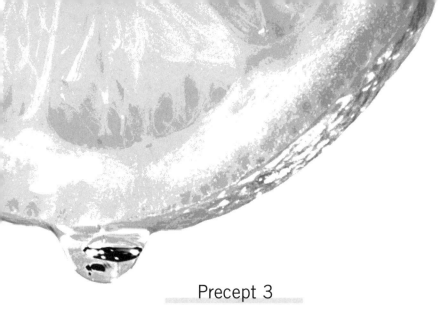

Do Something You Don't Want to Do— That Needs Doing

FOR THIS GOD IS OUR GOD FOREVER AND EVER;
HE WILL BE OUR GUIDE EVEN TO THE END.
PSALM 48:14

Balance your checkbook. Pay bills. Clean a closet. Purchase new tires for your car. Return a phone call to that difficult person. These and other mundane tasks usually come to mind when we think of the things we don't want to do that need doing. But beneath the merely annoying are the dreaded—those things that make your heart pound, your palms suddenly turn wet and your mind scramble for an easy solution.

Perhaps you have a broken relationship in your life that you want to repair, a letter of apology you've been putting off, a person with whom you need to have that crucial conversation. These tasks also need to be tackled and completed, even though you may not feel like doing them. But when you do them, oh the freedom you will experience and the peace and joy that will flood your soul.

Some of these opportunities present themselves in the moment, spontaneously, when you're not looking! Yet you recognize them when you see them, and you know intuitively the time is right to do that thing you don't want to do—the one you should do. It's now or never. So you roll up your sleeves, pray for the grace you'll need, and then you *do* it! And joy washes over you like a new spring rain!

I hope you enjoy a shower of blessings from the stories in this section. You'll read about a woman who discovers how organizing her life—even though it takes some discipline—not only blesses those around her but also transforms her own life. Letting go of being right brings unexpected joy to a woman who apologizes to a stranger, despite the cost to her pride! A grandmother sets aside her worry in order to be there for her granddaughter. A mother releases her son after another disappointment and embraces what God has for her in this situation. Two women talk about what has kept their marriages safe and healthy for 50-plus years. And finally, a woman lets go of a lifetime of fear and shyness when she decides to face these emotions.

Clutter's Last Stand

Marcia Ramsland walked through the family room, kitchen, living room and bedrooms. Toys, clothes, books, dishes, newspapers and magazines were scattered everywhere. She plopped down on a chair and dissolved in tears. "God, what's going on? My life is out of control."

She spent some time praying and then reached for her Bible. During the next couple of hours, she searched out 23 verses in Proverbs about the diligent and the sluggard. What a surprise to find that God had a lot to say about slovenly habits and lazy attitudes!

A passage from Proverbs 31 really got her attention: "She watches over the affairs of her household and does not eat the bread of idleness" (v. 27). Marcia felt the sting of recognition. She knew that she could not escape what God was showing her. *I have to get organized,* she told herself, and she committed that day to doing whatever it took to bring order to herself, to her household and to her family.

That event took place nearly 20 years ago. Today Marcia is a professional organizer, president of her own business, Life Management Skills, and a consultant to families and business owners. She is a Golden Circle member of the National Association of Professional Organizers in the United States. Marcia makes house calls and office visits to help individuals and companies bring order and peace to their environment so that they can live full lives that are satisfying and honoring to God and to themselves.

One of Marcia's favorite Scripture passages speaks to the changes that were a hallmark in her life and has inspired and motivated those she helps: "Who is wise and understanding among you? Let him show it by his good life, by deeds done in the humility that comes from wisdom" (Jas. 3:13). Marcia believes that even the most disorganized woman can learn new behavior. She knows—because she was once a "messy" herself!

Marcia's years of helping others organize their lives, their time, their paperwork and their homes are really an outgrowth of her study of God's Word. "The secular world I work in doesn't realize these lifestyle principles were given to us by God Himself," she says. "In fact, the world is amazed at the practical wisdom I share, but I'm not. Our God promises to give us wisdom, and I count on it every day."

Many participants in Marcia's seminars do recognize her spiritual approach, and they appreciate it. "I especially like the fact that you stressed the importance of spirituality and family over and above organizational skills," one woman wrote on the seminar evaluation sheet. "This truly matters most, and it will motivate me to unclutter my life."

"God will not take us where He has not prepared us," says Marcia. She responds to His call with courage, and she inspires other women to do the same. When you have a case of "I don't want to do it but it needs doing," consider following Marcia's proven action points. They are easier to practice than you might think.

• *Be generous with your time and expertise.* For example, donate a few hours a month to a nonprofit organization, or contribute your business products or services to a raffle or giveaway in your community.

- *Create a schedule that works for you and your family.* Marcia realized that when she conducted three seminars a week, her household suffered. However, when she cut back to two, she found that she could manage her business and her home with ease. It's important to have the support of your family. Plan together what works for your particular situation. For example, Marcia asked her son Mark how she could be more helpful. He told her that he would like to have dinner on time—at 6:00 as they used to. "Not 5:30 or 6:30," he said. Then he'd know how much time he had to do homework, practice his music, and so on. "Managing his time is important to Mark," says Marcia. "As his parent, I want to support him, so I agreed."

- *Commit your time and your life to the Lord.* "Keep in mind," says Marcia, "that you are not building your home but His; not your career but His." Remembering this will help you remain open to what God brings into your life or what He takes from it.

- *Read your devotions daily—no matter what.* Marcia recalls that in the past when she skipped her morning reading, her entire day changed. "I found myself regretting so many of my interactions," she says. "Now, each morning I write a new verse in my daily planner—the one that God gives me during my devotional time. I refer to it throughout the day, especially when things get rough!"

- *Focus on improving your habits and disciplines.* In other words, keep moving toward excellence. For example, at work, return phone calls promptly. Initiate opportunities that make good business sense (networking, business meetings, one-on-one time with prospective clients) and strive to exceed your customers' expectations. You can do the same at home. Listen to your family. Anticipate their needs and find ways to work together to achieve a harmonious home life.

It takes so little to be above average as you relate to your family, conduct a meeting at the office, participate in a neighborhood party or help your child with a school project. Don't allow clutter and chaos to rob you of the joy of being a truly godly woman. Get organized—God's way—and the rest will fall into place.

Action

Take a moment to visit Marcia's website, www.organizing pro.com, for help with simplifying your life and getting rid of the clutter. You can receive her free tips each week.

Reflection

Lord, I want to be a servant, not a sluggard! Please show me today how to put into practice Your mandates for living an orderly and peaceful life that will be a reflection of Your love and joy for everyone to see.

Inspiration

"If you live and work in an orderly way, you will think in an orderly manner."

—Marcia Ramsland

Highway Encounter

I knew I had made a mistake the moment I pulled onto the rain-soaked freeway crossing. It was foggy, the area was unfamiliar to me, and I was in a hurry. I thought the on-ramp to the freeway going north was on the right, but suddenly I saw that it was on the left. I looked over my shoulders hurriedly to check for oncoming traffic, and then I swung across two lanes to the extreme left and stopped. The light was red.

Just then, a huge motorcycle roared up next to my driver's window and lurched to a stop. The driver bounced in his seat from one leg to another, his dark eyes glaring at me through wide goggles. My heart pounded. *Where did he come from?* I wondered. *This lane was clear when I checked a moment ago. Or was it?*

I remembered how quickly I had cut over to where I wanted to be. *How did I not see him?* I froze in my seat, terrified that I had scraped the side of his bike or nicked his leg. He muttered something I couldn't hear through the roar of his engine and the sound of the traffic. I started to roll down my window, then stopped. *What are you thinking? You must be out of your mind*, I scolded myself. *Look at him. He's a bear of a man, covered in black leather. Why didn't he watch where he was going?*

"God, *please* turn the light *green*," I prayed.

A knock on my window snapped me to attention. The "bear" was screaming at me, shaking his right paw while gripping the motorcycle bar with his left one. ZOOM! VAROOM!! The bike screamed as this hulk revved the motor.

"God," I begged, "make it green. Are You listening?"

Suddenly, I saw myself doing something I didn't expect to do, didn't want to do and was panicky about doing. I opened the window halfway and looked the bear straight in the eye.

"Lady, get off the d— road if you can't drive," he screeched. "You nearly killed me. You got that? You cut me off, you got that? You and all the other gray heads are a menace to the road, you got that?"

"Got it," I said as bile rose in my throat. I thought I'd vomit on the spot. My heart hammered in my chest. And still the light was red—blood red. *A gun*, I thought. *What if he finishes me off right here? There'll be blood—my blood—all over the car, all over the street.*

"Green, God, please . . ."

Still the light was red.

I tried to talk my way through it. "I . . . I didn't see you," I whimpered, leaning on each word like a cane, trying to prop myself up before I passed out. And then the unexpected spilled from my lips. God knew what I needed to do, even though it took me a moment to catch up with Him.

"I'm so sorry," I said to the driver. "Will you forgive me?"

What are you saying? my mind screamed. *He's a jerk, an ugly, mean freak who hasn't got a drop of compassion. Why are you asking for his forgiveness?*

Because I was wrong, I shot back. *I was wrong.*

I looked up. The light was *green*. I was okay, still breathing. The bear zoomed off. My heart quickened with gratitude.

My mind settled down. I don't know whether he forgave me or not. He didn't say, and it didn't matter. I asked God to be with the bear as his helmet and boots and cycle disappeared into the rushing traffic.

I drove home, grateful for my life, for God's protection and for this experience. I didn't like what happened. I hope it will never happen again. But I'm glad it did happen so that I could do what needed to be done and learn from it, even though I didn't want to at the time.

Action

What can you do this week or even today that needs to be done even though you don't want to do it? Change the oil in your car. Apologize for a mistake that caused harm to another. Write thank you notes for gifts received. Pick one—and do it. Notice how you feel afterward. Then talk to God about this. What did you learn about yourself from this experience?

Reflection

Dear God, You know my list of things that need doing that I don't want to do. Yet I'm aware that I'll feel so much better if I do even one thing. There is nothing I can't accomplish today as long as I have You in my corner!

Inspiration

"The unexamined life is not worth living."

—Socrates

Thin Ice

I'll never forget my tenth birthday. My father came home early from work and picked me up at school, his new black leather ice skates slung over his broad shoulders and my new white ones in his hand. "We're going down to the pond to skate," he said, "just the two of us. It's my birthday present to you."

The mere thought of having my father all to myself brought tears to my eyes. He worked long hours in those days, and it was rare that he took time off for leisure.

I waved good-bye to my friends and jumped into our old tan car. Off we went to the nearby pond, now frozen hard after a week of freezing temperatures. I laced up my skates, wrapped a wool scarf around my neck, pulled my stocking cap over my long brown hair and donned my mittens. Then, hand in hand, Dad and I skated over and around the pond all afternoon. Whenever I hit a bump or felt scared, he was there, stretching out his hand to hold me up and to guide me through the maze of skaters whizzing by.

As the sun began to set, we piled into the car and drove home, our noses red and our cheeks cold. But our hearts were bursting with warmth—for one another, for the fun we had, for the celebration of my tenth birthday. I skated many times after that, but none meant as much to me as that special day I had with Dad alone.

One day many years later, one of my granddaughters invited me to her tenth birthday party. The afternoon would include lunch at a favorite restaurant and indoor ice skating at a local rink.

I said yes to lunch but no to skating! "I haven't skated in 45 years," I told Sarah. "I'd be scared to go out on the ice after such a long time. But I'll have fun watching you and your friends from the bench."

"Grandma, please don't say no. All my friends want to see you on ice!"

I laughed, picturing myself packed in frozen cubes up to my neck. "I'll think about it," I told Sarah.

For the rest of the week I wrestled with what to do. *You're not a sit-on-the-sidelines kind of grandma!* I told myself. *You're a tree-climbing, mountain-hiking, tag-playing grandmother.*

I wanted to skate. But I was afraid. Back and forth I went: yes one day, no the next. The Saturday morning of the party I made up my mind! I would get out on the ice and see what happened.

Sarah was thrilled when I told her my decision. When it was time to skate, I gulped hard and held on to my granddaughter's hand for the first round and then on to the guardrail the second time around. Within minutes, I felt my legs and feet strengthen beneath me. No more wobbling! I took a deep breath and stepped out into the whirl of skaters. "If only Dad were here with me," I whispered. I swiped at the tears that trickled down my cheeks. Dad had died the previous summer.

"Oh, Lord," I prayed, "help me do this. For some reason I really want this victory." Before I uttered the last word I realized I was skating—really skating. The more confident I felt, the faster I went, round and around, excited by this newfound freedom. Soon I was smiling, and then laughing.

I worked my way out to the center of the ice and began twirling and back-skating. I was feeling quite proud of myself when suddenly down I went—hard. How embarrassing! A teenaged boy in an orange vest zoomed across the ice, shouting for all to hear, "Ma'am, ma'am, are you all right? Should we call 9-1-1?"

By now Sarah and her friends were crowding around me. It was quite a show. They got their wish. They had seen Sarah's grandmother on ice! I could imagine making headlines in the local newspaper: "Spectacle on Ice: Fifty-Something Grandmother Steals the Show."

I pulled myself together, stood up on shaky legs, brushed the ice from my fleece pants and whispered, "No, I don't need 9-1-1. I was on skates before you were born. *Please!* Just give me a minute to recover."

The girls were giggling at this point, and I joined in. I wondered if at that very moment the Lord was chuckling, too. *Every time I step out in pride, there's a price to pay,* I thought. But when I reach for His hand *first,* I can skate through life with hardly a bump or scratch.

Even when I forget who's in charge, He gently reminds me—with a smile, a tug at my heart and a hand to grab.

Pride vanished as the truth of God's promise in Isaiah swept across my mind and encouraged my spirit: "For I am the LORD, your God, who takes hold of your right hand and says to you, Do not fear; I will help you" (Isa. 41:13).

I was renewed in that moment. If He would uphold me in a simple thing such as ice skating, surely He would be there for all the big challenges in my life as well—the things I wanted to do and the things that needed doing even when I didn't feel like doing them.

Action

Is there something you'd really like to do but you've held back out of fear, worry, anxiety or resistance? Ask God for the grace to push through the barriers and to do what you don't feel like doing that needs doing so that you can build your character and be a blessing to others.

Reflection

Dear God, please help me today to identify at least one thing that needs doing that I don't want to do—something that will help me grow as a woman and as a Christian.

Inspiration

"We grow because we struggle; we learn and overcome."

—R. C. Allen

Shifting Gears

The kitchen phone rang as I was about to light the candles and fill the water glasses. Our festive Christmas Eve meal would be ready in minutes. As I reached for the receiver, I glanced at the clock on the table beneath my telephone. It read 3:00.

"Hello. Merry Christmas," I said.

"Hi, Mom. It's Jim."

I knew something was wrong the minute I heard my son's voice. Then came the excuses. My teenaged son, who was living with his dad at the time, wouldn't be with us for Christmas Eve—or Christmas Day, for that matter.

I felt like lashing out at him. I was so tired of his last-minute cancellations. Whether a holiday meal, a picnic, a birthday party or Mother's Day, he couldn't seem to make it. But instead, I took a deep breath, whispered a prayer for wisdom and responded in a calm voice.

"I'm disappointed," I said. "And I have to admit, I'm hurt that you waited until the last minute to call. I'll miss you. You add so much to our gatherings. We'll all miss you."

He knew. He was sorry. But he just couldn't work it out. The reasons were familiar. What did it matter which one he used? He was not going to be with us.

My husband walked into the kitchen with questioning looks as he listened to my side of the conversation. Then my daughter got on the phone and gave her brother all heck. I took the phone back, wished him a happy holiday, told him I loved him and said good-bye.

I tried to hide my emotions from our other guests, but I know I didn't do a very good job of it. I was suddenly in tears. I hated the way I was feeling, but I couldn't seem to change. Then I became just plain mad. *Here was another example of what happens when there's a divorce,* I thought. Things will never be right again.

As I finished whipping the potatoes and stirring the gravy, I had time to pull myself together. I remembered what an older and wiser friend once told me: "Your parenting in the flesh is over. Your son is a young adult. Now your role is strictly spiritual. Pray for him and release him to God. He knows what to do, and He'll do it."

I mulled over my friend's advice once again and sighed in relief. I knew it was time to do what I did not want to do—now or ever: let my son off the hook! I wanted him to suffer—at least a little—for the hurt he had caused me time after time. But then I stopped. *What kind of mother am I? Wishing ill on my very own child, my only son, the young man I love with all my heart?*

I prayed again, asking God to release my pride and self-centeredness. Who was I to talk about being hurt when I had hurled years of hurt and sin at God and didn't think much of it until the day I knew that I was a sinner and needed a Savior. Everything had changed then. And everything could change now in this situation with Jim—if I simply let go. And so I did. I gave my son to God. And I relinquished my hold on him so that the Lord could do His will in Jim's life.

During the weeks following Christmas, I called my son, chatted, told him I loved him and never again brought up the disappointment I had felt when he phoned on Christmas Eve. Neither did he.

Through prayer and reflection, I began to see that the best thing I could do for myself and for Jim was to be a "love finder" instead of a "fault finder"—to be quick to locate the good in him and to affirm it. I'm grateful to say it worked.

In the years since, Jim has spent almost every Christmas with my husband and me. I remember him saying recently, "Mom, it just wouldn't be Christmas without being here with you and Charles. You always make it fun and relaxing. I go home happy, no matter what's going on in my life."

My heart leapt at his words. God had equipped me to help my son turn from isolation and self-centeredness by showing him my love, regardless of the circumstances. As a result, I have turned away from judging. Not only is Jim now an important part of our annual gathering, but he also actually participates in the church service, the singing, the praying, the laughter and the *joy*. He and I have become the best of friends as well as mom and son.

Action

Have you allowed someone to steal your joy? Have you backed away from doing in this relationship what you know needs doing but you don't want to do? It's not easy to confront and even disengage from a friend or family member we love when his or her behavior is damaging to us, but sometimes it's the very thing that brings healing. Pray about this, and if you have such a person in your life, ask God to show you what action to take and for the grace and strength to take it.

Reflection

Dear God, today I need a wagonload of courage and trust so I can speak up in situations that are damaging to myself and others. Please lead me one word at a time.

Inspiration

"We could never learn to be brave and patient, if there were only joy in the world."

—Helen Keller

FOR I AM THE LORD, YOUR GOD, WHO TAKES HOLD OF YOUR RIGHT HAND AND SAYS TO YOU, DO NOT FEAR; I WILL HELP YOU.
ISAIAH 41:13

A Hand to Hold

Lucy had been fearful and shy most of her life. She remembers as a child panicking as she rode in her friend's family car during an outing. *What if we get in an accident?* That evening when they returned to Janie's house for a sleepover, she lay in bed afraid. *What if I don't wake up? What if something happens to Mom or Dad while I'm away?*

Fear clung to Lucy like a trembling puppy throughout her early years—until one weekend at Girl Scout Camp the year she turned 13. "On Saturday morning our leader said we could tromp through the creek as long as we wore our rubber boots to keep from cutting our feet on the rocks," she recalls. "The other girls donned their boots and jumped right in. I stood back, watching and wishing I had their courage. I looked at the water rushing downstream and was instantly afraid I'd be swept away."

Next, the leader told the girls they could use their pen knives to whittle a twig into a piece of sculpture. Lucy was afraid she'd cut her hand. "I was afraid to help build the bonfire," she says. "I was afraid to perform in a skit. I was afraid to lead the group in song, even though I had a nice voice. No matter what occurred, I had some reservation about it."

The first evening at camp, when Lucy crawled into her sleeping bag, she feared waking in the night to go to the spooky outhouse at the end of a long dark path behind the sleeping lodge. "It had a hornet's nest in the corner, and there was no light inside," Lucy recalls. "I felt restless all night, tossing and turning in concern. I wanted so much to be a real part of this weekend, to put away the fear and shyness that kept me separated from the other girls. But I didn't know how to do it.

"Then, just as I had feared, I woke up in the middle of the night. I knew I wouldn't be able to hold out till morning. I'd have to take that dreaded path to the dark outhouse."

Lucy wiggled out of her sleeping bag and slipped into her sandals, trying not to awaken anyone around her. "My heart raced," she says. "Then suddenly a gentle hand touched my shoulder."

"Lucy, is anything wrong? Can I help?"

It was the Scout leader, Mrs. Quinn. Lucy burst into tears at the sound of her voice.

"I have to go to the bathroom," she sobbed. "But I'm scared to go alone."

"Of course. I understand," Mrs. Quinn said softly. "I'm scared, too. In fact, I need to make a trip there as well. Why don't we go together?"

Mrs. Quinn grabbed her flashlight with one hand and Lucy's hand with the other, and off they went.

"A feeling of peace and calm came over me during that short walk," Lucy recalls. "The stars sparkled and crickets chirped softly in the darkness. A sliver of moon shone overhead and a cool breeze wafted through our nightgowns."

"Isn't God good to shine His light on our path?" Mrs. Quinn said as she gazed at the bright crescent overhead. "He said He'd never leave us or forsake us. Imagine that! He is with us even on a path to an outhouse!"

"She grabbed my hand," Lucy says, "and we skipped the rest of the way. Even the hornets seemed to know they had no power to scare us that night. I can't explain what happened next. I just know something happened. My fear evaporated like raindrops in a summer wind."

After the two returned to the lodge, Mrs. Quinn tucked Lucy into her sleeping bag and kissed her forehead. "Thanks for being my midnight companion," she whispered. "God bless you. Sleep tight."

"I did sleep tight the rest of that night," says Lucy. "I woke up smiling! Something had changed. I knew it. I made the most of that last day at camp. I tromped through the stream with the other girls, and I perched on a sturdy branch to whittle a piece of wood with my new knife.

"I knew then that fear had lost its grip on me. Mrs. Quinn had given me her hand when I needed it. That experience encouraged me to reach for other hands during the years and to offer mine to people in need. Eventually, I discovered the one hand that can keep me safe from fear forever: the hand of God."

Action

Everyone has fear. What is yours? Choose the Scripture verse at the top of this story or one of God's other promises regarding His protection from fear. Write it out, personalizing it with your name. For example:

> You [insert your name here] *will not fear the terror of night, nor the arrow that flies by day* (Ps. 91:5).

Place this verse on your mirror or desk or dresser so that you can say it and receive it each day.

Reflection

God, I pray right now in Jesus' name that You will remove the terrors that plague me day and night and that You will hold me in Your mighty hand in all my trials.

Inspiration

"Fear is the main source of superstition, and one of the main sources of cruelty. To conquer fear is the beginning of wisdom."

—Bertrand Russell

Loving for a Lifetime

I pulled the invitation from the envelope. *How special*, I thought, as I read the inscription. We were invited to a dinner party at the home of our friends Corinne and Ed. It would not be an ordinary gathering, however. It was to be a celebration of the couple's fiftieth wedding anniversary. What a milestone! We didn't want to miss it. I was sure we could learn a few things from this amazing couple who had made it to the half-century mark.

When we arrived on the night of the party, we were escorted to the garden where tables were beautifully decorated with fresh flowers, colorful tableware and pretty napkins. Festive punch, hot appetizers and warm conversation added to the pre-dinner hour. Before and after the meal, we sauntered through the couple's home, taking time to look at photos of Corinne and Ed and their children at various stages in their family life. Their wedding album was displayed on the coffee table in the living room. Everyone crowded around, curious to see what they looked like and what they wore on that special day five decades before.

I was deeply moved by this unique evening of tribute to two people who model commitment to all who know them. Sometime later, I asked Corinne what kept them together, what she felt the secret ingredient was that helped them sustain their long marriage and still remain interested in and devoted to one another.

"Making sure the Lord comes first," Corinne was quick to say.

More than anything else, Corinne's relationship with God has helped her maintain the balance she needs to keep going when times are rough. "Whenever we face difficulties, we stop and remember how God has taken care of us in the past," she says. "He's been with us through difficulties again and again. He has proven Himself worthy."

Corinne says that when she and Ed recall this truth, they're better able to take a deep breath and carry on, even in the dark days when two sons were diagnosed with cancer, when one separated from his spouse, when there were difficulties with in-laws and challenges at work.

Fifty years with one person is a long time! Yet the years become sweeter as they accumulate, Corinne added, because of the intimacy that comes through shared history, creating a family together, nursing one another through hurts and illness, laughing together and making decisions and choices with the other one in mind. Corinne rated a sense of humor high on her list of traits that help one keep a positive perspective!

Ed counts himself a "blessed" man. To him, Corinne is the "best" wife. He "upholds" and "cherishes" her. For some people, such words sound old-fashioned. But every woman should be so graced! Ed's devotion to Corinne was never more evident than at their anniversary party when he wrapped her in loving words and looks during his toast to his bride.

Pretty awesome—after 50 years!

Another couple I admire recently celebrated 55 years of wedded life. How did they do it? "I gave up my right to be right," declares Barbara Jean. "I learned the hard way, by watching my mother-in-law press her rights with my father-in-law while they were living with us, and one day I suddenly realized, I'm just like her. I do the same thing with Vic."

Barbara Jean said she decided then and there to give up her right to be right! "I realized that Vic is just being who he is. He's not trying to hurt me or fight me. And when I began to see him in that light, I saw what a precious person he is."

Barbara Jean went on to share how that insight has changed all of her relationships. "We each have our own point of view on life," she added. "I now see that most marital problems really have very little to do with one's spouse. We get upset because we think *our* way of doing things is the *right* way or the *only* way. But it's not. The other person has his or her way, and it's just as valid as ours."

Barbara Jean is spontaneous and bubbly. Vic is methodical and quiet. But together they make a beautiful whole! After all these years of living together, growing, changing, leaning on God and seeing one another through ups and downs, both admit they wouldn't want anyone else. Barbara Jean and Vic. Like peanut butter and jelly, one just isn't the same without the other!

Corinne and Ed and Barbara Jean and Vic admit they didn't always want to take the high road, but they knew that they needed to if they were going to keep their marriage strong and loving over the long haul. Both couples agree that often our concerns are motivated by selfishness. *We* want this or that. *We* don't like this or that. *We* wish this or that about our spouse would change. But when we bring these feelings to the Lord first, He can minister to us and to our mates before we hurt one another with damaging words, emotional outbursts or regrettable actions. If He is first in our life, then we can pray over the big things, smile over the little stuff and keep on loving over a lifetime, able to do what we sometimes don't feel like doing but know we need to for the greater good of our relationship.

Action

Consider what you have done or could do to enhance your relationship with your spouse, to display your love day after day for a lifetime. Is there something you can give up or take on that will help bring this about? Pray to discover it, and then do it.

Reflection

Lord, please help me today to assess my own behavior instead of evaluating my spouse's. Show me how to lean more on You and less on my own willfulness.

Inspiration

"To love deeply in one direction makes us more loving in all others."

—Anne-Sophie Swetchine

Precept 4

Do a Physical Exercise

THE EYE IS THE LAMP OF THE BODY. IF YOUR EYES ARE GOOD,
YOUR WHOLE BODY WILL BE FULL OF LIGHT.
MATTHEW 6:22

Exercise means different things to different people. Some women break into a sweat at just the sound of the word! The thought of sit-ups, squats and crunches is enough to wear them out before they even consider joining a gym. For others, it's as much a part of their daily routine as brushing their teeth or feeding the dog.

I doubt that Aunt Grace had aerobics or bench pressing in mind when she wrote this precept. But she did know the importance of challenging our bodies if we're going to have a balanced and joy-filled life. What you do is, of course, up to you. Perhaps for you, a small plot of dirt for planting tulips or tomatoes is your exercise field. Gardening is your game! Or you may enjoy, as I do, a vigorous hike in the hills, followed by a short nap beside a stream.

Whether you bounce, jump, skate, lunge, swim, walk, jog, weed your garden or vacuum the carpet, physical exercise is part of what will keep you going and feeling good. You might want to combine exercise with another activity as well to pass the time creatively and productively.

Need an incentive to start? Read the following stories. For example, did you know that kissing is a way to keep fit? And how about prayer walking or fishing and hunting? You'll meet three women who discovered these creative ways to exercise. And what about shaping up by throwing stones or cleaning your house? Inspiration is just ahead.

Fat Lips

Rachel's husband, Rich, came home from work one night and laid one on her—a smash-mouth kiss—right there at the door. Then he handed her a box of chocolate kisses. "Rache, it's time we got into kisses again—chocolate and otherwise," he said, lifting his brow with a hint of romance. "We're rushing too much. We need to take time for each other, to be close again. I miss kissing!"

Wow! Rachel didn't know what to say, so she opened a piece of the silver foil-wrapped candy and popped it into her mouth. *I thought we were into kissing.* Rachel kissed Rich when he left for work each morning, and she kissed him when he arrived home at night and again before dropping off to sleep. Kiss! Kiss! Kiss!

But now that Rachel thought of it, her kisses were more like peck, peck, peck! A peck on the cheek. A peck on the lips. A peck on the top of Rich's head. *Hmm. He has given me something to think about.* And think about it she did.

Then Rachel jumped online and did a "kissing" search. She found a neat little article titled "The 20-Second Kiss" on the Bottom Line Secrets website:

The 20-second kiss can revive the feelings that brought you together. A long, slow, deliberate kiss—

which need not progress to further sexual activity—can be a great reviver of closeness. Simply agree that either of you can ask directly for a 20-second kiss when feeling underloved or underappreciated. *Also helpful:* The 60-second hug. Use it to say good-bye or to reconnect after a busy day. About halfway through a long hug, you will relax in each other's arms and feel a great release of tension.[1]

Rachel popped a couple more chocolate kisses in her mouth and savored their sweetness while she read the "secret" again. That evening she noticed a magazine on the coffee table with an article that encouraged people to exercise their lips. As people age, the article stated, their lips become thin. The author's answer to thin lips? Kissing, of course!

Within a few minutes, Rachel had a wealth of new information on a topic she hadn't given much thought to. *Wait till I show this to Rich. He'll love it.* Then she thought better of handing him the articles. How romantic is that? "Honey, here's the latest scoop on the health benefits of putting our lips together!" No! She needed to *demonstrate.*

The next morning when Rich was about to walk out to the garage, Rachel stopped him at the door. "Hey, where's my kiss?"

Rich *blew* Rachel a kiss. She couldn't believe it. No lip-to-lip contact. *After his request for more kissing just the night before and after all the research I did on Google, he* blows *me a kiss? No way, mister.*

And with that Rachel pressed her lips against Rich's and felt his warm, sweet breath overtake her. Rachel lingered for at least 20 seconds, though she didn't time it. That would've been tacky! Then Rich got into it, and they must have gone over the limit by a good 5 seconds. Ahhh! No chocolate kiss can take the place of a real one with the man you love.

Rich smiled, lifted his brow in that romantic way of his, and opened the door. "Bye, Rache," he whispered, and then he was gone.

Rachel ran to the mirror. Sure enough, her lips were fuller already—and her heart as well!

I can get into this! she thought.

Action

Kissing is good for the soul, for the heart, for the mind, for the spirit and for the body. Practice kissing today. Kiss your spouse long and often. Kiss your children and grandchildren, parents and siblings. There may be a time when one or more is not there to kiss, so start today so that you will have kissable moments to remember later on.

Reflection

Paul reminds us, Lord, to greet one another with a holy kiss. May I keep that in mind today when I am with family and friends. Help me to pay attention to the moment rather than watching it pass by and then regretting when it's too late.

Inspiration

"People who *throw* kisses are hopelessly lazy."

—Bob Hope

Note

1. "The 20-Second Kiss," *Bottom Line Secrets,* January 15, 1999. http://www.bot tomlinesecrets.com/blpnet/article.html?article_id=136510 (accessed August 28, 2005).

Prayer Walking

Jody looked at herself in the entryway mirror. She let out a long, slow breath. She tried to picture what she had looked like 20 years before. Not easy. She headed for the laundry room. It was Saturday afternoon. Her husband, Jeff, was golfing.

"I should be out swimming, sailing—anything but washing clothes," she scolded herself.

She glanced out the window. The grass needed mowing. The fridge was nearly empty—enough that she could see the glass shelves were due for a good wiping.

But she couldn't muster enough energy to do any of it. Not a good spot to be in for a mother of three teens. Jody knew that she had to get a grip on herself. She wanted to lose weight, to look at life in a new way, to shed the depression that had plagued her most of her 42 years. She had read about the benefits of walking—plain and simple walking—not power walking or running or jogging, just putting one foot in front of the other for one hour each day.

She had promised to start—last month, six months before that, two years ago! The phone rang, snapping her out of the funk. "Jody, Sue here. It's such a beautiful day. Want to meet for a walk and a lemonade afterward? My treat."

Jody took in a deep breath. "I'm in the middle of . . ." She stopped short. *In the middle of a pity party is what you're in.* The little voice inside sounded accusative—in a playful sort of way. She laughed out loud.

"What's so funny?" Sue asked. "Clue me in."

"I'll tell you when I see you. Meet you at the park gazebo in 20 minutes, okay?"

"Okay."

Jody and Sue walked for an hour and then cooled down over a lemonade.

"We should do this more often," Sue said as they hugged good-bye. Jody nodded. She wanted to say yes, but she'd disappointed herself too many times before.

On Sunday, during church service, she asked God to help her make a commitment to herself to *walk*. That was it—no diets or pills or half-promises. She started the following day.

A week later, Jody noticed that she felt better and was actually ready to get out of bed in the morning, eager to watch the sun come up, to hear the birds and to smell the sweet aroma of fresh hay in the field behind their ranch house. She felt brave enough to set a goal she knew she could keep: one hour of walking five days a week at dawn, rain or shine, at home or on vacation.

Pretty soon her husband, Jeff, noticed the change.

"Hey, what's your secret?" he asked over dinner one night. "You're smiling more. And you seem . . . well . . . more energetic! Are you on some kind of pill?" He frowned as though suspicious.

Jody told him what she'd been up to, and she invited him along. That week they began walking together each morning. When they came home, they fixed breakfast as a team and said their prayers.

One morning later that week, they were both in a hurry. Jody suggested they pray as they walked so that they wouldn't have to give up either activity. "That started an entirely new routine," Jody told Sue when they met for an afternoon walk a few weeks later. "Prayer walking. We've been doing it ever since."

Sue wanted to know more.

"We don't carry a list of prayer needs or plan what we'll say," Jody said. "We let God guide us. Sometimes we focus on our family or our marriage, and some days we feel the weight of the world, so we pray for what's going on here and abroad. Other times we pray for someone we see on the street, such as a homeless person, a mom jogging with her baby in a stroller or a teen on a skateboard. Some days we pray for the farms around here and for the shops in town."

"You're amazing," Sue said. "You've inspired me. I'm going to tell Alan about this."

Jody walked home, thinking about how walking and praying had changed her life during the past few weeks. She was ready to go shopping for some new clothes, a size down from the past. She laughed when she remembered the woman at the hair salon who asked if she'd had a face lift.

"Yes," Jody had joked. "And it didn't cost me a dime. I'm lifting my face each day in prayer!"

Jeff resolved difficulties at work, neighbors cleared up financial challenges, and farms in the area prospered. "I can't take credit for any of it, Lord," she whispered as she put the key in the lock and entered the kitchen. "The results are entirely Yours. I'm beginning to understand what you meant when you told us to pray without ceasing."

Jody thought about how little television she and Jeff were watching these days and how good they both felt when they went to bed early and slept well. She loved knowing they were in this together, building their schedule around prayer instead of trying to fit prayer into a packed schedule.

On their next walk, Sue asked Jody how they handle distractions. "What if you run into people you know as you walk and pray?" She and her husband had started prayer walking, but they were struggling with getting sidetracked.

"We include all of it," Jody replied. "We may chat for a moment and then pray for that person when we part. If we get sidetracked or go off on a tangent, we don't worry about it. Sometimes our conversation, especially if one of us needs to talk something out, is a prayer in itself. God does not require a certain format. He simply wants us to talk to Him—to bring Him all our needs and concerns, our joys and victories."

Sue reached for Jody's hand. "Thanks," she said. "I feel better just talking to you."

Jody and Sue finished their walk, set another date and waved good-bye as they went their separate ways. When Jody arrived home, she walked in the front door and paused in front of the mirror. She giggled at her reflection. She liked what she saw and the way she felt. "Walking with You, Lord, has its perks. Thank You!"

Action

Put on your walking shoes and see where they take you. Grab a friend, a spouse, a child, your dog or go by yourself. Prayer walking will take you on a journey to joy and good health!

Reflection

Lord, please give me the desire to get out there and pound the pavement in prayer for your people, for my family, for the world and for myself.

Inspiration

"Walking is man's best medicine."

—Hippocrates

Matching Vests

"Ned was the most handsome man I ever saw," said Marion. "When I see him now, lying in this hospital bed, frail, white as the wall, hardly knowing me, I could cry."

"Tell me about him," said the nurse as she propped up Ned's head and urged him to take a sip of water.

Marion brightened at the memory that pushed its way to the front of her mind. There she sat, age 17, on the bank of the old fishing pond in Riverside, Illinois. Ned nestled beside her, pole in one hand, as he slipped a wiggling worm on the hook at the end of the line.

"Wanna try?" he asked, smiling in a way that hooked her!

The nurse tapped Marion on the shoulder. "Are you all right?" she asked.

"Oh my, yes, fine. I got lost for a minute thinking about days so long ago."

Marion settled back in the chair and began talking. "We met in high school," she said. "I know that some people don't believe in love at first sight, but I do, 'cause it happened to Ned and me."

"When did you marry?" the nurse asked.

"Two days after my eighteenth birthday. Ned was 20." Marion laughed and looked away for a moment. "Daddy had a fit. Said we were just a couple of crazy kids. But he didn't stop us, so we made our plans. We got married in the community church and rented a small studio apartment six blocks from where I had grown up. Close to my mother and father, but not too close, if you know what I mean."

Marion got up, walked over to the side of the bed and stroked Ned's head. "He was such a darling man," she said. "Still is, though he can't show it now like he used to."

Marion opened her purse and pulled out a frayed photo of Ned. He was wearing a T-shirt and dungarees and his hair was black as licorice. He was leaning against a Chevy convertible as though he owned the world.

"He was handsome," said the nurse. "Sounds like you were both lucky to have one another."

"I know I was," said Marion. She sat down on the edge of Ned's bed and stroked his slender hand and then pressed it to her cheek.

"Some of my friends thought he controlled me," she added. "But that's not true."

The nurse adjusted the pillow under Ned's head and tucked the blanket under his chin. "What made them think that?" she asked.

Marion leaned forward as though she was about to share a carefully guarded secret. "Well, for a wedding present he gave me my own rod and reel," she said and laughed. "And for my birthday the following year, he gave me a shotgun for hunting. That was more than 40 years ago."

She looked up and smiled, waiting for a reaction. "Not very romantic, I admit, but later I realized that both the gun and the pole gave me a unique opportunity to enter my husband's world, to learn more about him, to spend time with him. Isn't that why I married him? To be with him. And what better way than to share his interests?"

Marion was aware that other men often left their wives behind to pursue their outdoor hobbies, but Ned wanted his wife to share these experiences with him. "Hunting and fishing were also good ways for us to keep ourselves fit—together," she added.

"After receiving and learning how to use these gifts, it was my turn to surprise Ned," said Marion. "I blew him away on our first anniversary with HIS and HER fishing vests and caps and license holders with safety pins to fasten to the vests! Certainly a new fashion statement for me.

"We've tromped all over the country searching out the best fishing holes. We've cast our lines into farm ponds and cool mountain streams in West Virginia and Kentucky, from ocean piers in Florida and Georgia, and around the oil rigs in Lake Pontchartrain in New Orleans. I never became great at fishing, though I did land a trophy fish once. But most important, I became an expert at sharing my husband's life—and I kept my weight under control with all that walking and crouching and lugging our boat and gear and pitching tents."

Marion mused on those days, then added, "I've received many romantic gifts from my husband over the years, but none have brought more meaningful memories than my rod and reel."

The nurse touched Marion's shoulder. "I'm about to cry," she said. "What a touching story."

"I look back with much joy," said Marion. "We made the most of what we had when we had it. And now I have a mind filled with beautiful memories, especially of our special weekends hunting and fishing together."

Marion stared out the window for a moment. "In today's world, feminists would have a field day with my story," she said. "I can almost hear the comments and questions. 'Why didn't he enter her world?' 'Isn't this just one more example of how men suppress and manipulate women?' Could be, for some. But I chose my man and I chose how to live my life with him. It was more important to me to be with my husband than to hold on to an idea of how a marriage should be. It was different, all right! It was wonderful and I have no regrets."

Marion stood up, kissed Ned's forehead and wrapped her arms around the nurse. "Thanks for listening," she said. "I feel blessed all over again."

Action

What physical exercise would you like to do with your mate or a good friend? Take an action that will help you and the other person have fun staying fit together.

Reflection

Dear God, today please help me work my body and my spirit for good health and good fun.

Inspiration

"A bear, however hard he tries, grows tubby without exercise."

—*Pooh's Little Instruction Book* (inspired by A. A. Milne)

Throwing Stones

Are you having a bad day? Not just a bad *hair* day—but a bad *work* day? Do you feel like kicking the desk, cussing your boss, firing the airhead who polishes her nails when she's supposed to be entering data? Go ahead, let off the steam—in your mind or in the ladies' room—when no one's around! God will listen. He can handle your frustrations. He might even agree with some of them. Go ahead; ask Him.

Then grab a pen and paper and write down as fast as you can all the people, situations and feelings you want to get rid of. Don't think too hard. Just take 'em as they come. Next, put a number in front of each one.

1. Anger
2. Disappointment
3. Airhead Annie
4. Lost promotion
5. Stupid decisions
6. Confusion
7. Art's indifference
   and so on . . .

Put the list in your purse or briefcase. On the way home, stop somewhere (the park, the lake, the beach, the side of the road) and pick up a bunch of stones or rocks. Not just any old stones—be selective. Pick one to represent each item on your list: a big gray one for that lost promotion, a white one with gold flecks for Airhead Annie, a craggy stone for confusion. Keep going until you have as many stones as you have items. Mark each stone with the corresponding number.

Then pitch those stones down a ravine with all you've got, throw them into the lake or wield them as far as you can across a vacant lot. Ahh! You'll feel so much better after throwing stones. It's incredibly cathartic. It's not enough to *think* the bad stuff away. It doesn't leave. It hides in the corner of your mind collecting dust. Then when you least expect it, it comes out to get you. Better for you to get rid of it *now*—with an action that satisfies the mind and the spirit.

Don't let the principalities and powers in the unseen world keep you stuck in anger, jealousy, disappointment or confusion. Give each one the heave-ho! Then sit down and take a big gulp of air, allowing the fresh wind of the Holy Spirit to fill you anew.

Action

Collect your stones, mark them, and pitch them. Today! Better to do this by yourself in a safe place so that you can put your whole body into it. Ahh! What sweet release. Sometimes words won't do. Only throwing stones will.

Reflection

Lord, help me to toss rocks and stones instead of relationships.

Inspiration

"The true test of walking in the Spirit will not be the way we act but the way we react to the daily frustrations of life."
—Beverly LaHaye

In Praise of House Cleaning

Feather duster. *Check.*

Sponge mop and tile cleaner. *Check.*

Furniture polish and rags. *Check.*

Glass cleaner. *Check.*

Rubber gloves. *Check.*

Vacuum. *Check.*

Bucket, brush and toilet bowl cleaner. *Check, check, check.*

No getting around it now. I had everything I needed. It was time to roll up my shirt sleeves and clean our condo. I started in the living room.

What should have taken about 30 minutes took an hour. I got lost in the watercolor paintings on the wall. I lingered over each one, remembering the artist as well as the circumstances that led us to purchase them. The lovely landscape by my friend Elisa Gittings, the desert scene by Georgianna Lipe, the exquisite rendering of Rock Creek in the Sierra by Lady Jill Mueller.

I chuckled as I thought about my taste in art *before* I met my husband, Charles. It certainly has moved to a new level since then. Together we have visited art galleries, museums and local art displays from New York to Los Angeles during the past 20 years, and our home is now a small museum of our own, displaying the many pieces we fell in love with.

Next I vacuumed the furniture and the carpet. I stopped from time to time and examined each item closely, as if for the first time. I'm grateful for the choices we made—the beautiful colors and textures, and I'm thankful for the money to buy them. Lord, you brought those funds to us in the nick of time!

As I continued from one room to the next, my eyes filled with tears. Every item I touched had special meaning. DVDs and videos brought music and viewing pleasure to our lives. Our stove and oven and sink and disposal and fridge and water filter assured us of moment-by-moment convenience and sanitation—something two-thirds of the world will never enjoy, including those in the border towns of Mexico, not far from our home.

I moved from the kitchen to the den and then to my office, touching, dusting and straightening books, family photos and small collectibles, appreciating in a new way the people behind the scenes: the artists, the craftsmen and craftswomen who wove our carpet, put together our computers, built our furniture, laid the tile and installed our appliances.

I swished the toilets, thankful to have not one, but two. I spritzed the windows and enjoyed the view of the San Diego Bay across the street and the trees in the yard with huge magnolia blossoms. And I stood beneath the simple wooden cross hanging over our front doorway, aware that it was Jesus who made this life possible for me, not by anything I did, but by His sacrifice on the cross.

I stood back and observed what I had accomplished within a few hours. Our home sparkled. It smelled fresh.

It felt good to the touch. And I had exercised my body and spirit.

I gathered my cleaning tools and put them away.

Feather duster. *Check.*

Sponge mop and tile cleaner. *Check.*

Furniture polish and rags. *Check.*

Glass cleaner. *Check.*

Rubber gloves. *Check.*

Vacuum. *Check.*

Bucket, brush and toilet bowl cleaner. *Check, check, check.*

And one more thing. Thank You, God, for the physical strength to do this work. Now I see house cleaning as a prayer as well as a task. It's good for our home, it's good for my body, and it's good for my soul.

Action

Walk around your house or apartment and take stock of what you have and how each item has blessed your life. Recall where each item came from and what it means. Then clean and dust and wash and straighten. You'll feel great, and your home will, too!

Reflection

Oh, God, I thank You for these gifts of furniture, carpet, window coverings and so much more. You have provided, and I am grateful.

Inspiration

"Out of the strain of the Doing, Into the peace of the Done."

—Julia Louise Woodruff

Do a Mental Exercise

I WILL PRAY WITH MY SPIRIT, BUT I WILL ALSO PRAY WITH MY MIND;
I WILL SING WITH MY SPIRIT, BUT I WILL ALSO SING WITH MY MIND.
1 CORINTHIANS 14:15

Crossword puzzles, brain games, books and magazines and such are all ways to exercise our minds. I love to read. But lately I've rediscovered the fun of playing cards and board games. When Charles and I get together with family or with friends, we bring out the deck and sit around shuffling and dealing, winning and losing, talking and laughing our way through hours of fun. We enjoy one another as we engage our minds. Even the youngest ones begin to strategize how to win the game.

But we can also exercise our minds through memory, if we take the time to do so, and through the words of other people as they speak their wisdom into our lives, and by simply being present to another person, sometimes in an unexpected way. Such a trip is worthy of our time to see what to keep and what to toss, what to embrace and what to leave behind.

I hope the stories in this section will offer you inspiring ways to exercise your mind. You'll read about the legacy a grandfather left to his granddaughter, a way to expand your vocabulary by adopting new words and making them your own, a man's gift to a writer who influenced his life, a fairytale princess who discovers the difference between controlling and being controlled and, finally, a woman who realizes she's a liar.

Walking Dictionary

One Tuesday afternoon following New Year's Day, I began putting away the holiday decorations, the crèche, the ornaments and the paper chains our grandchildren had made for our tree. It was a bittersweet time. I was ready to close out the old year and open the new. I was filled with nostalgia and anticipation at the same time. I knew what I was leaving behind but unsure of what lay ahead.

I opened the glass doors of the antique bookcase that stands in the entryway of our home to return the porcelain figurines of Jesus, Mary, Joseph and an angel to the top shelf. As I was about to close the case and lock it securely, I decided to take a few moments to scan the many beautiful items on each shelf—delightful and delicate reminders of the past: my bronzed baby shoes; a lovely handmade quilt my mother-in-law, Ada, had made as a young woman; my father-in-law's razor; the metronome my husband had used when learning to play the piano; a beautiful gold bracelet my father had given me years before; a hand-painted dessert plate passed on to me from my grandmother's collection.

I fingered a few things, lingering over these treasures that tied me to my heritage. At the back of one shelf, I noticed a worn volume, held together by a fading blue binding. I recognized it immediately as the *Webster's Collegiate*

Dictionary my grandfather had given me for my eleventh birthday. I pulled it out, my hands shaking as I held it close.

I sniffed the aging paper and was transported immediately to a time more than half a century ago when I opened it for the first time and shouted, "Grandpa, thank you! This is just what I wanted." His blue Irish eyes smiled back in delight. I'm sure the book cost a significant part of his small pension check that week, but I'm also sure he didn't mind. He was devoted to me, his first grandchild, and wanted the best for me in every way.

A puddle formed in my eyes and I blinked it back as I opened the crumbling volume and saw again his lovely handwriting, still clear and bold. A shiver of joy slid down my spine as I caressed the page that held his inscription.

Dear Karen,

Many happy returns on this your 11th birthday. With the good start you have already attained in the expression of meaningful words, I am confident that with the help of this book, you will soon become a walking dictionary.

Love, Grandpa

I smiled and then chuckled out loud. *So like Grandpa,* I thought. I could almost hear the lilt of his voice in the words he wrote. Grandpa knew who I was and what I was meant to do long before I was certain of these things myself. He was right. Here I am more than 50 years later writing, speaking and mentoring aspiring writers. Words are what my life is about. Words spoken in prayer. Words on a page within the covers of a book. Words of correction and encouragement on a student's manuscript. Words of apology. Words of blessing. Words of praise. Words of inspiration from a platform. Words of gratitude in my journal. Words of joy each morning as I wake up to a new day.

It would be easier sometimes to march down the hallway of life without so much as a glance to the right or to the left, to what's ahead or to what lays behind. I could shut off my mind to the pain and the sin, the embarrassments and the disappointments. But if I were to do that, I would also close off the possibilities and the opportunities to transform my life by renewing (and exercising) my mind. And so I continue on, savoring, sharing and saluting life with words.

"You were right, Grandpa. I am a walking dictionary."

Action

List three things you might do to renew your mind (start a journal, read a book you wouldn't usually be drawn to, create a photo album and scrapbook of your childhood, and so on). Pick one and start today.

Reflection

Lord, God, I want to renew my mind starting right now. Help me to think on those things that are true, noble, right, pure, lovely, admirable, excellent, and praiseworthy [see Phil. 4:8].

Inspiration

"Reading is to the mind what exercise is to the body."

—Sir Richard Steele

THE QUIET WORDS OF THE WISE ARE MORE TO BE HEEDED
THAN THE SHOUTS OF A RULER OF FOOLS.
ECCLESIASTES 9:17

Adopt a Word

On January 1 of each year, I adopt a word and make it mine for the next 12 months. We are together full-time, my word and I. So I'm fussy about the one I choose. It has to be a good fit. It has to feel like me, and it has to be big enough to take my attention away from competitive words like "no" and "can't" and "won't."

One year I chose the word "praise." I kept a praise journal that year. By December 31, after writing praise notes to God for 12 months, I was a different person. My life became a celebration of praise instead of a cacophony of complaint. I was aware of God in a way I had not been before. Now I want everyone to know Him and to realize how worthy He is of praise.

Praise the LORD, O my soul, and forget not all his benefits (Ps. 103:2).

Another year I picked the word "gratitude." That, too, has earned a high place in my hierarchy of transformational words. I continue to utter it each day, even though it is not the word of the year. I have so much to be thankful for. How could I ever let it go?

00008116996

The year I chose the word "joy," I found myself living in a more joyful state, simply by choosing to. Amazing—the power of one word! I no longer wait for people or places or things to bring me happiness. I choose to be happy. I dwell in joy.

This year my word is "peace." I want to be filled with it, regardless of the circumstances. As a result, I am moving at a slower, more deliberate pace, taking time to *experience* each action, to *be* with the people in my life—from family and friends to my students and strangers. I'm eating and sleeping and reading and walking and talking and thinking in a more peaceful state than ever before. I want to hand out peace like candy kisses—to sweeten someone's day and mine as well.

And the peace of God, which transcends all understanding, will guard your hearts and your minds in Christ Jesus (Phil. 4:7).

Sometimes I succeed and sometimes I fail miserably. Last week, for example, I had a speaking engagement at a church located about 45 minutes from home. It should have been a breeze to drive to the site. But it wasn't, due to an overturned crane on the freeway. It took 90 minutes to reach my destination. As I sat in my car, crawling along at 1 mile per hour, I thought a lot about my word—"peace."

I decided to stop holding it as a thought and to practice living it. I couldn't control my situation, frustrating as it was, but I could control my attitude. So I flipped on the radio to a station that plays classical music and allowed myself to relax into it, to enjoy the beautiful scenery outside my window—snowcapped mountains in the distance and deep green hills after the rainstorm from the week before.

It soon became clear that I would not make it to the event on time. I phoned the meeting planner and told her my dilemma.

"Don't worry," she consoled. "I'll just flip the program around. What we were planning for the last half, we'll do first. That will open the last half of the morning for you to speak."

Thank heaven for cell phones and for compassionate meeting planners! I arrived with a moment to spare—just enough time to visit the ladies' room and freshen my lipstick. My topic for the day was "Finding joy in everyday life—regardless of the circumstances." Hmm!

I took a deep breath and plunged into the subject, and within seconds, all residue of frustration fell away and I was at peace—and in joy!

The book of Isaiah in the Old Testament records the following:

The work of righteousness shall be peace; and the effect of righteousness quietness and assurance for ever (32:17, KJV).

"Peace"—a living word for today and every day of my new year!

Action

Spend a few moments considering a word that you would like to adopt. Look up its meaning in the dictionary and do a word search in the Bible. Pray over this word, and ask God to show you ways to practice it in your life today and all through the coming year.

Reflection

Dear God, I want my life to reflect the meaning of Your words. Help me to be an example of joy and peace and gratitude and love in the lives of everyone I encounter today.

Inspiration

"Until you make peace with who you are, you'll never be content with what you have."

—Doris Mortman

Bob's Gift

An elderly man tapped me on the shoulder. "Excuse me," he said. "I've been trying to get to you all day." He approached me in the lobby of a hotel during a break from a conference we were both attending. "Are you Karen O'Connor? Someone said you were."

"Yes, I am," I replied.

"The same one who wrote that article for *Reader's Digest*, 'The Best Gift We Can Give'?"

He really had my interest now.

"Yes again," I said, curious as to where this would lead.

"Well," he said hesitating, "you packed a whollop! I did not like it one bit when you wrote something about how we owe it to other people to participate in the joyous and the solemn occasions of their lives—that it's almost a duty to be there for them. *Be there*," he repeated with a touch of sarcasm. "Isn't that the phrase you used?"

"Yes," I said, backing away. I imagined he was going to haul off and slug me at any minute. I felt my pulse escalate and my joy dribble out like water from a punctured can. No one had ever confronted me—in person—about my writing. He even remembered some of the very words I had written. I didn't know what to say. I began doubting myself. Maybe my editor had been wrong about the focus of the article. He was the one who encouraged me to write on a topic I felt passionate about.

"I want people to finish reading your article, put down the magazine, get up and take action," my editor had said, "not merely read your words and then turn the page to the next article." Obviously this man was taking action—but it was against me. I don't think that's what the editor had in mind.

"Sir, I'm sorry my words offended you," I said, trying to hold on to a smile. "But I stand by them. I feel strongly about the importance of people being there for one another. I don't think any of us realizes how much our presence matters." I lowered my voice, hoping to engage his softer side.

Then I stopped, realizing I was defending myself. *You don't owe him or anyone an explanation,* I told myself. *No one can steal your joy—unless you allow it. You have the right to your opinion, and he has the right to his. End of discussion.*

"Thanks for letting me know your thoughts," I said lightly, trying to sound polite, "but I need to get back. It's almost time for . . ."

"Don't you want hear the rest of my story?" he asked. I noticed a bit of a smile break through, even though he appeared to be holding it back.

"I'm sure it's very interesting," I said, pulling away, "but right now I'm . . ."

"It worked," he called after me. "I didn't like what you wrote . . ." He was nearly shouting now, his tone high-pitched and determined. "But you were right. I tried what you said—and it worked." His voice boomed over the dispersing crowd.

I stopped midstep and turned toward him. "Why don't we walk back to our seats together?" I said in a hushed tone, "And you can finish your story as we go."

He laughed. "Got your interest now, don't I?"

"As a matter of fact, yes, you do," I said. I couldn't help smiling. This curious little man had captured my affection. *What is he up to?* I wondered.

"Well," he said, "I finished reading the article, mulled over your words and by the time I finished your check-list—you know, be positive about invitations, if possible go out of your way to attend a graduation or a funeral or whatever, and the one about making amends if you can't make it in person."

I couldn't believe what I was hearing. He remembered my article better than I did.

"Well, when I finished reading, I got right up from the sofa, grabbed the phone and called my brother, Eric. He was planning a family reunion in June—last June, matter of fact, and I was invited, of course. Never been to one before. He keeps having 'em every few years and I keep saying, 'Sorry, can't make it.' I hate those big shindigs—noise, gossip, kids running everywhere. It's not for me. I live a quiet life. Never been married. Like to do things my way."

I got the picture.

"But something happened after I read that article. Something inside changed," he said in a softer voice. "I got to thinking about my duty. Some of those kids don't even know they have a great-uncle. Never seen me before. And I've never seen them. And my brother—well, he's in his late 70s now. I hadn't seen him in 10 years or more."

We were nearing our seats at that point. "I'll get right to it," he said, chuckling. "I told my brother I'd be there—and I meant it. I went, and it was one of the best things I've ever done."

I saw tears in his eyes—but just barely—because now my eyes were filling up, too!

"So, you did a good job," he said. "You wrote what you believed in, and it got to me. Thanks. I wish you could have seen those kids. They were all over their great-uncle Bob. That's me! Never felt so happy in my whole life."

I reached out and put my arms around Bob. He hugged me back.

Words weren't necessary. We were both living the article. We were being there for one another.

Action

Is there someone who needs you to be there for him or her? How can you meet that need? It might be as simple an action as an encouraging word or a loving gesture. Decide today to make yourself available to at least one person in a way that requires something of you.

Reflection

Lord, I get caught up in my own life and often forget that other people could use a helping hand, a listening ear or a caring word from me. Please help me today to look beyond myself and to be there for someone in need.

Inspiration

"A gift, with a kind countenance, is a double present."

—Thomas Fuller

Diary of a Princess

Princess Lucinda remembers well the day when she felt
> abused
> accused
> used-up
> upside down
> down right mad
> sad and
> *had*—all at the same time.

She had tried to be nice, but what good did it do? The more she said, the worse it became. And the worse it became, the more she said—and did, until she did herself in! She opened her diary and scribbled out her feelings till not a word was left.

Then something wonderful occurred. That very day she happened on a book that featured the writing of another princess who, just like her, was up to her eyebrows in being *nice*. Princess Adora had scrawled across the pages of *her* diary the following words:

> NICE is as cold as ice, *not*
> as warm as spice
> as people in my kingdom would prefer me to
> think of it.

They had much to gain by her niceness, she continued.
They liked it when she
> shut up
> shut down
> held back
> backed off
> backed away
> backed down
> *and*
> buttoned her lip!

So she did—except when she wrote in her diary each
night before falling asleep.

Princess Lucinda realized that if *she* didn't speak up for
herself, she might be stuck in *Nice* forever, just like Princess
Adora. She couldn't imagine such a fate, especially when
she didn't deserve it. All she had ever wanted to do was
please the people around her, but it hadn't worked. No
matter how hard she tried, afterward she felt as though she
were dying. People didn't thank her for being *nice*. They
didn't respect her for being *nice*. They didn't appreciate her
for being *nice*.

> Being *nice* isn't safe.
> It isn't fair.
> It isn't fun.
> It isn't real.
> It doesn't help.
> It didn't heal.

So she went to the King. "I don't like it here," she complained. "I feel
> unhappy
> unwelcome
> unappreciated
> unchallenged

unmotivated
under the pile . . .
undone!"
The King lifted her chin and looked into her eyes.
"Come to me and I will give you rest," He said. "I'll carry
your burdens, for my yoke is easy. Peace I leave with you;
my peace I give you. Be still, my princess, and know that I
am God. I never asked you to be *nice*. I asked you to be
truthful and kind and *real* and to follow me."
Princess Lucinda wept in gratitude. She realized how
she had brought all this unhappiness on herself. "I have
tried my best to please others, to solve their problems, to
take care of them, to advise and help . . ."
"And *control*," added the King.
Oh no! *Control?* She thought she had merely
       spoken up. Then when it didn't turn out as she
          hoped, she
       shut up and
       sucked it up.
And where did that leave her?
       Uptight!
       tied up in knots
       not knowing what to do next.
Had she tried to do what only the King can do?
Was being nice
       just another way
       to have her way?
       to have her say?
       to control, console and extol
       for her own glory?
Now she felt
       tongue-tied
       shell-shocked

defrocked
thunderstruck
and stuck!

"Seek first *My* kingdom," said the King, "and I will add the rest. My purpose is to give you life in all its fullness. Everything you need I will give you—and more. I love you with an everlasting love."

Princess Lucinda sagged against the bronze door of the palace and *breathed.* Then she smiled at the King and touched the hem of His robe with reverence.

"Thank You," she said, "for setting me free—from me."

Action

Write a page in your diary about how you have compromised your life for the sake of approval. If you don't have a diary, start one today. Pour out your feelings to the Lord and ask Him to guide you into His truth.

Reflection

Dear Lord, I see myself in Princess Adora and Princess Lucinda. Please help me today to give up control, to stop kidding myself about how and why I try to manage myself and other people. I surrender control to You and ask You to guide my steps and order my day.

Inspiration

"We cannot always control our thoughts, but we can control our words."

—Florence Scovel Shinn

Lies

My cell phone rang as I pulled into a parking space in front of the supermarket.

"Hello. This is Karen."

"Hi, Karen. I hope I didn't catch you doing something important."

I didn't recognize the voice, but the woman's tone was friendly, so I responded. "Just picking up a few groceries," I said. "Who's this?"

"Lonnie," the woman replied. "Remember me? I met you on a hike last year."

Lonnie. Of course. Instantly I recalled her face and her infectious laugh. I juggled the phone with one hand and turned off the ignition with the other. "How nice to hear your voice," I lied.

I really was too busy to talk. I was making dinner for eight. The guests were to arrive in less than three hours and I still had a batch of cookies to bake.

"I'm starting a home-based clothing business," said Lonnie. "I'm going to introduce the line to some of my friends at an introductory party next Saturday afternoon. I'd love to have you join me. It would be a great chance to see you again."

My throat tightened and a knot formed in my stomach. The last thing I needed was another invitation. My husband and I had promised we'd slow down over the summer and make more time for one another.

I felt torn. I know how hard it is to start a business. I wanted to say yes so that Lonnie would feel supported. At the same time, I wanted to say no so that I wouldn't disappoint my husband. Then I thought of a third option—a lie, actually. I'd tell her that I'd call her back after I checked my calendar—even though I already knew the state of my calendar. Still another idea occurred to me. Say yes, and see how it goes. Maybe it would work out. I could always call and cancel the day before.

Lies, lies, more lies! I thought. *Why couldn't I just tell the truth? I can't make it! I don't need to explain myself. Even the dinner party was based on a lie. I offered to host our card club when I knew I was overtired and not in the mood for cooking or baking.*

I tossed up a prayer for help, and God delivered the grace I needed. "I can't make it," I said. But I didn't stop there, even though I should have.

"Wish I could," I added and blabbed on about coming some other time and maybe even helping her set up. *There I go again,* I realized. *Another lie. I don't wish I could go. I don't want to go some other time. The truth is, I'm relieved I'm not going. I hate home product parties.*

Lonnie's voice invaded my selfish thoughts. "I understand completely," she said. "We are all so busy. Take care and have a lovely weekend," Then she was gone.

I felt like a worm. I wish Lonnie had begged me or laid on a guilt trip. I might have given in. But no, she was kind and sweet. I heard generosity in her voice. I was the one who was deceitful. I pretended to be interested when I wasn't. I acted as though I wanted to attend when I didn't.

By the time I hung up, I was a wreck. An incidental phone conversation had turned into a lesson in mental and spiritual integrity!

What is with me? I wondered as I walked up and down the aisles of the supermarket. *Why do I cut corners to avoid looking bad? Why do I say yes when I really mean no?*

I drove home, unloaded the groceries and sat myself down. Then I picked up my daily devotional from the coffee table and leafed through it, hoping some page would speak to me. I remembered having read something about boldness the week before. Ah! There it was in black and white:

A life of holy boldness demands more than merely getting by. It requires that we keep our word. It's a duty in the highest sense—to God, to ourselves, and to others. When we say what we mean and then do what we say, we honor the Lord, show respect for others, and lay a foundation of accountability in our own lives that keeps us faithful to God's truth regardless of the circumstances.

The verse for that day hit me hard:

In everything set them an example by doing what is good. In your teaching show integrity, seriousness, and soundness of speech (Titus 2:7).

Soundness of speech—I wasn't exactly famous for that! The words reminded me of a time several years ago when an elderly neighbor was quite ill. I had promised his wife to stop by to chat and pray, but I never did. Occasionally I left a card or a flower at their door. My gestures were kind, but my words were empty. I hadn't done what I'd said I'd do.

Then one morning I discovered a note under my front door. "Last night at 10:30, Karl went to heaven." The words hit me like a lead weight. I had not kept my word, and now it was too late.

A few days later, I met Karl's wife in the lobby of our apartment building. "Phyllis," I whispered. It was the only word that escaped my lips. As our eyes met, we reached for one another like two children. We went to Phyllis's apartment, and in that next hour, her pain became mine as she talked about her dear husband. I realized that God was giving me another opportunity. This time I took it. Phyllis and I talked and prayed over tea, and I went home a changed woman.

I know that sometimes I don't keep my word because I can't. Something happens. I plan an event—and suddenly, there's a death in the family. That happened when my father died, and I had to rearrange my schedule. One time I promised a friend I'd care for her children so that she could attend a party, but then I came down with the flu and had to cancel. Or the time I signed up to be on a planning committee at church and then realized down the road that I had overcommitted myself and couldn't go through with it.

I am learning—slowly—that guilt and embarrassment make the problem worse. If I can't attend the event or honor the commitment, I can still go to the person, explain what happened and ask forgiveness if that's appropriate. Perhaps I can take on a lesser job or reschedule the commitment. The important thing is to tell the truth humbly and with care.

I opened my journal and scribbled a quick note to the Holy Spirit.

*Hold me accountable, please. Stop me in my tracks when
I start to fudge, dodge, turn away and just plain lie!*

I closed the book and prayed for yet another chance.
I see that I'm only as good as my word. And my word is only
as good as the Word of God on which I stand.

Action

Commit today to making your yes, yes and your no, no.
Practice so that you will form a habit. Pray for guidance so
that you can hold on to it.

Reflection

*Dear Lord, I want to say what is true, whether it be yes or no so that
I can become a person of integrity in mind, body and spirit. Please
lead me in the path of righteousness so that I will devote my thoughts
to what is pleasing in Your sight.*

Inspiration

"Truth is the only safe ground to stand on."

—Elizabeth Cady Stanton

Precept 6

Look for Joy in Unexpected Places

MAY THE GOD OF HOPE FILL YOU WITH ALL JOY AND PEACE
AS YOU TRUST IN HIM, SO THAT YOU MAY OVERFLOW WITH
HOPE BY THE POWER OF THE HOLY SPIRIT.
ROMANS 15:13

Looking for joy suggests taking the initiative, not merely responding to a joyful situation, but being actively engaged in locating and experiencing it. Looking for joy in unexpected places adds another layer to the task. It suggests that we go after joy aggressively, looking for it, creating it and embracing it, even in a place where we would not generally find it, where we would expect just the opposite.

The stories in this section are examples of just that—looking for and finding joy in the underbrush of life, in the dark and sad places, in any and every situation, because where God is, there is joy! You will meet a young woman who discovers what it means to share the Lord's joy with the poor, another who finds happiness in giving in to silliness, one who experiences bittersweet joy when laying a parent to rest, a woman's experience with a neighbor who turns a hurt into a healing, and a new way of looking at one's self that can bring renewed joy.

HE WHO OPPRESSES THE POOR SHOWS CONTEMPT FOR THEIR MAKER, BUT WHOEVER IS KIND TO THE NEEDY HONORS GOD.

PROVERBS 14:31

A Home from Heaven

The Martinez family was destitute. They had lost everything they owned in a fire: the paper and cardboard hut they called home as well as their meager possessions—a cooking pot, a makeshift bed, sleeping mats, food, blankets, boxes for chairs and their only table. By the time a missions team from a church in Southern California arrived in Tijuana, Mexico, to help them, all they had were the clothes they were wearing.

But they had not given up hope. Mrs. Martinez had prayed for a miracle—a real home—one that would keep her family warm, dry and safe.

She knew that a home would not fall from heaven, but still she felt certain God would answer her prayer. So when she heard about an opportunity available to families like hers to qualify for a small house free of cost, she submitted her family's name to the team who builds homes for the needy, scarcely believing that people would actually show up and do the work.

When they did, however, she knew who had made it possible. God answered her prayer through the men, women and children from a church in the United States. They had come to Tijuana ready to do what they had promised.

It was an amazing event to observe. American and Hispanic volunteers of all ages worked side by side. Whether or not they could speak to one another in English or Spanish didn't matter. They had a more important goal in common—building a home for this family in dire need. People from neighboring villages also lent a hand. The men nailed the floor together, erected walls, laid the roof and wired the home for electricity, while the women and children grabbed brushes and buckets of paint.

Everyone over eight years of age joined in. Some people did the hard physical work, while others interacted with the adults and played with the children. The purpose was twofold: to erect a house and to share Christ.

College student Alison Slomka has been so touched by this ministry that she's joined the team seven times. As a result of this work, she also decided on her life goal: to serve the underprivileged as a nurse.

"I have learned the poor are not only those without money or homes," Alison says. "They are people without options. Only a relationship with God can transform their lives. I can be a tool God uses to show them His love and compassion."

Alison spent most of her time with the boys and girls. "I can speak Spanish decently," she admits shyly, "but I get nervous in front of adults." The kids didn't seem to mind if she made a mistake. "It was great to just chat with the kids while they helped us paint." She struck up a conversation by asking their names, their favorite color, what sports they liked and where they went to school. During the breaks, she and other young people played soccer with them.

During another weekend, the team built a house on a corner lot that was exposed to the street. The grandmother of the family got sick and ran a fever during the construction. Later the team learned the cause: She had been sleeping at night on a cement slab outside the house to protect the building materials from being stolen!

One of the most touching events of the weekend occurs at the end of the project. The team gathers around the house, prays over it, blesses the family and provides an opportunity for the family members to accept the Lord as their Savior or to reaffirm the faith they already have.

"I don't know if everyone could understand the full extent of the message we brought," says Alison, "but they listened." Others were already followers of Jesus Christ, and they knew He was the One who had provided their new home. "Most were in tears during our final time of testimony and prayer before we handed over the keys."

Only time will reveal the full impact on the families who received these new homes. As for Alison and the team, however, they received their reward with each nail they pounded, each stroke of the paintbrush and each smile of gratitude from the families they blessed.

They had gone to serve the poor and received far more than they expected. They found the joy of giving—in the trenches, under the hot sun and on the faces of the men, women and children who turned the key in the door to their brand-new home from heaven.

Action

What act of mercy could you take on behalf of someone less fortunate than you? Serve in a soup kitchen, visit women in prison, join a home-building team, go on a short-term mission? Consider your talents and options and then choose to become involved.

Reflection

Lord, I want to serve You by serving others. That is where I will experience real joy. Please help me today to discover the special role You have for me.

Inspiration

"Lead the life that will make you kindly and friendly to everyone about you, and you will be surprised what a happy life you will lead."

—Charles M. Schwab

Bolt out of the Blue

Words. I love 'em. My mother did, too. "I'm a word-person," she'd say as she worked her daily crossword puzzle. She found joy in talking, in writing, in helping me learn to spell and in reading. I inherited her fascination with language. In fact, my car license plate—WORDY—speaks to my love affair with words.

Today, as a professional writer, I think about words, as well as their meanings, a lot. Although I try to be original in my expression and provide readers with fresh images, I sometimes catch myself falling into a tunnel of clichés. Fortunately, there is light at the end of this tunnel, too, as well as a good laugh and lots of fun in this most unexpected place.

When I get started, it's hard to stop. I can come up with more clichés than *you can shake a stick at.* Then I remember that *this, too, shall pass*, even though at the time I find *it's as easy as pie* to *fall under their spell.*

My son Jim and I talked about this on his recent visit—since he, too, is a writer. We began trading clichés and couldn't quit. Our conversation was suddenly *a mixed bag* of time-worn phrases, and we didn't know what most of them meant or how they originated. Since then I've found some neat websites that provide the phrase and its origin and meaning, so at least I am now better informed when *I let the cat out of the bag* and start talking in clichés. I should *let sleeping dogs lie*, but what fun is that?

In fact, laughing at such silliness is one of the ways I remain in high spirits, keep my mind engaged and feel *as good as gold* and *as mellow as fine wine*. Oops! See what I mean? As much as Jim and I tried to *avoid clichés like the plague*, the more they sprang from our lips—and they're still springing!

After an hour or more of this tomfoolery, I vowed to be *as quiet as a mouse* so that I wouldn't add to the pile of phrases that was *growing by leaps and bounds*, but it didn't work. Soon I was *up the creek without a paddle, laughing all the way*. In fact, *we laughed till we cried*, but even the tears couldn't stop us. We were having *more fun than a barrel of monkeys!* I often wondered just how much fun that would be. Then I thought about what it means to be *as happy as a clam*. That one really *takes the cake!*

By that time, I felt like *throwing in the towel* or, more to the point, *throwing the book at myself*, the book of clichés, that is. On the other hand, if I did that, I'd be *a sitting duck, stuck in a rut* or, worse, *up a tree* and *madder than a wet hen*, worried that I'd gotten myself *in a pickle* with *more than I bargained for!*

Finally, I felt that I had said all I needed to say on this subject—at least for that day—so I decided to *beat it like a rug* before I *hit the point of no return*.

If this little story *rings your chimes*, let me know! I'll be *waiting with baited breath*. Or maybe to you, this is simply *much ado about nothing*. Either way, I'd love to hear from you. *Don't put off until tomorrow what you can do today*. *Bite the bullet* and send a note. I promise it'll be a *cake walk*. I want to assure you, however, that *the buck stops here*, so don't hold

back even if you decide to *send slings and arrows* my way.
A penny for your thoughts! Send your comments to karen@
karenoconnor.com. And remember *any friend of yours is a
friend of mine,* so *get off your high horse* and *cut to the chase. At the
drop of a hat,* tell a friend about your experience with clichés.

Then send your own *fresh as a daisy* prose to me. It'll *lift
your spirit* and *put a feather in your cap!*

Action

Check out some of the cliché websites through Google.com
and discover the meaning behind some of these time-worn
phrases. I promise an hour or more of pure fun. And if at
first you don't succeed, try, try again! Remember, the road
to success is always under construction.

Reflection

*Lord, I'm laughing my way through this silly exercise, but at the
same time, I'm realizing what fun it is to laugh. There is joy in letting go and not taking life so seriously. I know it's good for me to
look on the bright side! Oops! There I go again.*

Inspiration

"Any great truth can—and eventually will—be expressed as
a cliché."

—Solomon Short

Dust to Dust

Mother died peacefully in her sleep one October afternoon in a small bed in the nursing home where she was living at the time. I had watched her decline, month by month, over several years, after suffering a stroke and then gradually losing contact with the world and the people around her.

When my sister June called with the news, I wasn't shocked the way I would have been if she had keeled over on the golf course of a heart attack at age 45. But still, the news rocked my world. It didn't matter that Mom was 89 when she died and that she had lived a good long life, as friends are eager to remind one at such a time. Eva O'Connor was *my* mother. *My* life changed the moment I knew she was gone. I would not hear her voice again or feel the touch of her soft cheek against mine.

I threw some clothes into my suitcase and within a few hours, I pulled up in front of my sister's home. I took a deep breath to steady my nerves, set aside my feelings and shifted into gear. We had work to do—and June and I would do it together! We arranged for a memorial service followed by a small reception for family and friends, and then for cremation here in California and ultimately for burial in Chicago, Illinois, in a cemetery where our father and grandparents were already buried.

Everything was under control.

I was all right.

Until the day of the cremation.

Until I walked up the front steps of that 150-year-old crematorium.

Until I moved into the small room with the narrow table that held a long cardboard box containing my mother's body.

My brother and sister and I gathered around the table (our youngest sister had returned to her home in Italy, but we had her emotional support) as Father David, June's parish priest, said a blessing and led us in prayer. Then the mortician stepped forward and opened the box. He slipped the top to one side, just enough to expose our mother's sweet face and the top of the snow-white sheet that swaddled her naked body.

She had come into the world naked and alone until warm hands had cradled and swaddled her. And she was leaving the same way.

I clutched the arm of my brother, Kevin, and he reached over and placed his strong right hand over my trembling one. Then each of us took a moment to say good-bye to our mother—one with a kiss, one with a caress, one with a gentle touch to the wisps of soft gray hair that framed her peaceful face.

After one last look, we stepped back and the mortician replaced the top of the box and then signaled the assistant to ignite the furnace. Whoosh! The flames leapt from the burner as the mortician wheeled the table to the entrance of the chamber and slid the box into the vault. I watched in awe as the tongues of fire licked the sides of the box. Tears ran down my face, my legs wobbled, and my heart raced at the sight of my mother returning to dust before my very eyes.

"For dust you are and to dust you will return" (Gen. 3:19) proclaimed the Lord. What had once been my mother's body—the one that had given birth to me—would soon be contained in a small bronze urn.

The assistant closed the iron door and clamped the heavy handle in place. I looked once more through the small window of the vault, pondering my sister's wistful comment, "If I could deliver Mom to the gates of heaven myself, I'd do so."

We turned then, our family trio, and walked out of that cold room, down the steps and into the warm October sunshine. My heart ached. I felt unhinged.

I lifted my heart in a silent prayer of thanksgiving for my mother, for her life, for all she had meant to me and for all she had done for me. She had been my Girl Scout leader and my cheerleader—from spelling bees to piano recitals! She comforted me when I lost a best friend and encouraged me when I married and moved far away. She was at my side when I gave birth to my children, and she was there on the dark day when my first marriage ended.

Eva O'Connor had not been a perfect mother. This was no time to idealize or idolize her. But she had been the perfect mother *for me*. I knew she loved me. And I loved her.

I closed my eyes for a moment as I savored the memory of her. Then slowly a small bubble of joy worked its way up from my toes to my stomach, to my heart, to my mind, to my lips. *Praise You, O God,* I shouted within. *You have been Mother's Lord all the days of her life, even to her old age and gray hair. And now you have carried her into Paradise.*

My mourning turned to joy in that moment—at a most unexpected time in a most unexpected place.

Action

Consider a time in your life when joy burst through in a most unexpected place. Write a few lines in your diary or journal about how that felt and what it meant to you.

Reflection

Lord, only You can turn mourning into joy at times of loss and death. Thank You for this gift of consolation when I am in my greatest need.

Inspiration

"Learning to live in the present moment is part of the path of joy."

—Sarah Ban Breathnach

Seeing Red!

Day after day I strolled along the concrete walkway that leads from our condominium unit to the stairway. And each day I was annoyed by the sight of what appeared to me a bedraggled, overgrown plant drooping over the edge of the walkway above, down to the second floor where I live.

"Why don't they do something about that thing?" I said half aloud. "It's an awful sight and it's half-dead anyway. Why not prune it? The plant would thrive if this lonely tentacle weren't sucking energy from the main shoot."

I had it all figured out. If only the owner asked for my advice! But she didn't. I complained to my husband about it.

"Leave it alone. It's not your property."

"But it's unsightly," I argued.

"Don't look at it," he countered.

I should have listened, but I didn't.

One day I could no longer resist the urge to clip, clip! So I did. I reached over the railing with my pruning shears and snapped them shut around this ailing limb. It dropped into my free hand, and from there I sent it down the trash chute! I felt better—almost heroic. I had put this poor thing out of its misery.

I went on with my day, working at my desk, returning phone calls, responding to mail. In the late afternoon I went out to the post office. When I arrived home, I ran up the stairs from the parking garage and was suddenly stopped by the sound overhead of a woman crying. I then heard the soothing words of another woman, who appeared to be sympathizing with the first one. I looked up and there stood Leslie, my neighbor on the third floor. Her neighbor Nan stood alongside, arm around Leslie, as the two commiserated about the plant that had been mutilated by some uncaring person below.

My stomach went into such a knot, I can't describe it. I don't remember ever feeling so embarrassed and anxious in my life. I felt like a criminal. My heart pounded so fast, I could hardly talk. But I knew what I had to do. I had to confess or someone else in the building would take the rap for something I had done.

I set down the mail on the spot and ran upstairs, breathless. "Leslie," I said, "I'm the culprit. I'm the one who cut your plant. I'm so sorry. I should have asked first. Charles told me to leave it alone. It was your property. But I thought it would be okay to prune it a little since it was hanging over the railing all the way down to the second floor . . . and . . ."

I couldn't stop. I was mortified, embarrassed, apologetic and defensive all at the same time!

Leslie stood listening with eyes wide in disbelief. And Nan didn't know what to say. I stopped. And Leslie spoke. She told me how she had worked so hard to get that little plant going. It was finally thriving, and then someone just cut it off. She couldn't imagine why anyone would be so cruel.

Of course she was right. It was a cruel thing to do, even though I didn't see it that way at the time. I was so caught up in my opinion of what looks good that I took action, regardless of how it might affect another person.

I was off to a poor start on a day when I had wanted to do something nice and unexpected for another person! Unexpected, yes. Nice, well, not exactly.

I apologized profusely, wanting her to understand that I wasn't motivated by spite (though I wasn't sure at that point). I had just wanted to tidy it up a bit!

She thanked me for being honest and dried her eyes, and we parted. The rest of the day was pure misery for me, not so much because of the plant. I knew it would keep growing. I hadn't destroyed it. But I had hurt a neighbor, someone I like, a person who lived close by.

I couldn't let it rest. I prayed about what to do. Then I ran downstairs, jumped in the car and drove directly to the local nursery. I spent some time selecting a beautiful, thriving, flowering plant that looked similar to the one I had cut. I bought it, wrote a card, acknowledging my fault once again and asking for Leslie's forgiveness.

Within moments of leaving the gift at her doorstep, I received a call. Leslie accepted my apology and thanked me for such a thoughtful gesture.

Wow! I was stunned at how easy—and how difficult—that experience had been.

By evening I realized the day had turned out differently from what I expected or planned, but still, it had turned out. I had made things right—when I had been wrong—and in turn, my neighbor had done something for me. She gave me the gift of a second chance, an opportunity to feel joy in an unusual and unexpected situation.

That night I lay in bed reflecting on the great value of such a gift, so grateful for all the second chances God gives me each day. I take delight in the joy Leslie helped to restore in me, but even more so in the gift of eternal joy I have through Jesus Christ.

Action

Think about a time when you did something wrong but were too embarrassed or too scared to admit it—until the Holy Spirit quickened your mind and heart and you *knew* that you had to make things right. How did you feel after you resolved this incident?

Reflection

Dear God, how many times a day I disappoint myself by sinning against another—even in small ways. An unkind word here. A hurtful action there. But You are quick to forgive when I turn to You. Help me be swift in my confession so that I can receive Your grace once again.

Inspiration

"Joy is prayer. Joy is strength. Joy is love. Joy is a net of love by which you can catch souls."

—Mother Teresa

Girl with a Red Bow

From the time I was in third grade, I had wanted to be a writer of children's books. I loved books—the feel of them, the smell of them, the look of them. Trips to the library became my favorite outing as a child. It was a place of refuge. No one scolded me there. No one told me to sit up straight, to drink my milk or to kiss a maiden aunt who had a mole on her face with a stiff black hair poking out of it.

At the library people smiled. The lady behind the desk helped me find books just right for me. After checking them out, I remember skipping down the steps of the old building, a little girl with long brown hair and a big red bow.

I finished elementary school and went on to high school. I cut my hair and did away with bows. I was a young woman now. But life as a teenager was not a happy experience. I was small, physically immature, painfully shy and obsessed with trying to belong.

I graduated from high school and went off to college the following September. Life in a women's dorm was an adventure. I met new friends and felt a growing confidence as I discovered that I could live away from home and make it. Something else happened that first year, something wonderful but quite unexpected. I walked into the campus library and a warm and familiar feeling came over me. I felt once again like the little girl with long brown hair and a big red bow, safe in the boundaries of the library. I returned there every day to study, to read, sometimes just to walk among the books—to look at them and to smell them and to touch them.

I graduated from college and got married two weeks later. I left behind the little girl with the big red bow. I didn't need her anymore. At last I belonged. I was somebody's wife, and two years later, someone's mother. I did grown-up things like sewing and needlepoint, cooking, playing tennis with the ladies and teaching Sunday School.

But children and children's books became important again as I introduced my son and two daughters to reading during weekly visits to the library. Sometimes I tied up my daughters' long hair with a big red bow. And sometimes, with an armload of favorite books, we skipped down the library steps together.

Then my marriage ended in divorce nearly 20 years later, and everything I had loved and longed for seemed to end with it. I stopped going to the library. I stopped going to church. I gave away my sewing machine, threw away my yarn and needles and sold my tennis racket.

I moved to San Diego. I felt hopeful. Maybe life could be good again. I remarried a few years later. I returned to church. I discovered the mountains and the beaches. I found the library! I put aside the pain of the past.

But it came back when I least expected it. In the middle of what I thought being happy was all about, I was suddenly sad—about the past, about changes and choices I had made, about my children and my dog and my career and my parents and . . . well . . . about everything and anything.

This time it wouldn't go away. Not in church. Not in the mountains. Not in the library. Not at my typewriter. I entered private counseling and began the hard work of rebuilding my inner life. It became the journey of a life-time—deep pain, deep joy, deep truths.

After six years, my counselor and I agreed that we were nearing the end of our work together. It would soon be time to say good-bye. During our last few sessions, we recounted my victories and the things I had overcome.

On one occasion a most unexpected thing occurred. I began to weep. Then deep wracking sobs took my breath away. The tears were so great that I couldn't talk. *Where is this coming from?* I wondered.

My counselor encouraged me to close my eyes and let the feelings register. I did. And there in front of my mind was a picture so clear that it could have been hanging on the wall. I saw myself, a child in third grade, a joyful little girl with long brown hair and a big red bow, jumping up and down for all she was worth and shouting at the top of her voice. "You found me! You found me! I've waited so long."

Oh dear God, I thought, sobbing again. *It's me!* The mental image perfectly matched a picture of myself at that age hanging in my bedroom.

I began to sob again. I closed my eyes once more and there she was. But this time, she was sitting on the floor in front of me, her head in my lap, her arms curled around my legs. Then she looked up and said in a voice I will never forget, "You don't have to cry anymore. We found each other, and we will never be separated again."

What joy! What freedom! I had found *myself*. At last I truly belonged. Suddenly I understood the importance of getting to know that small person within. I believe that child is the keeper of the key to my heart.

Today, if you see me on the street, in church, at the supermarket, at a conference or in the library, you may recognize me on the outside as a sixtyish woman with gray hair, a grandmother. But don't let appearances fool you. I am really a little girl with long brown hair and a big red bow.

Action

What is your inner child saying to you? What do you have to say to her? Write down any conflicting feelings you may have about the person you are on the outside and the one who lives within. Ask God to help you recognize and embrace your true self—the one He created and loves.

Reflection

Dear God, I want to be all that I can be. Please help me today to find harmony within so that I can be my best self in all areas of my life.

Inspiration

"Getting in touch with your true self must be your first priority. "

—Tom Hopkins

Precept 7

End Each Day with an Original Prayer of Thanks

WHEN YOU LIE DOWN, YOU WILL NOT BE AFRAID;
WHEN YOU LIE DOWN, YOUR SLEEP WILL BE SWEET.
PROVERBS 3:24

Writing or saying an *original* prayer can be intimidating—if you're not used to it. Perhaps you're more comfortable turning to a book of prayers or reading from Scripture. There is nothing wrong with either one. But I encourage you, especially when ending the day, to do so with thanksgiving, to give your heart and mind and words entirely to

God. Simply talk to Him, sharing the highlights of your day, whatever they were, and then giving Him all the praise and thanks for whatever comes to mind—even the challenges or the events that occurred that you didn't like or that don't make sense. You can be certain that when you humble yourself before Him, acknowledging Him as the master of all, your heart will swell with appreciation; and when you are grateful, you cannot help but be joyful as well.

Following is a selection of spontaneous and original prayers of thanksgiving that I hope will encourage you to pray your own. There is a sample prayer for a blessing received, a problem resolved, a lesson learned, a decision made and a request granted. I hope they will ignite a passion for prayer within you so that you, too, will end each day with an original prayer of thanksgiving.

BE JOYFUL ALWAYS; PRAY CONTINUALLY; GIVE THANKS IN ALL CIRCUMSTANCES, FOR THIS IS GOD'S WILL FOR YOU IN CHRIST JESUS.

1 THESSALONIANS 5:16-18

Giving Thanks for a Blessing Received

Dear Lord, what a day! I woke up feeling scared and unsettled about money. Surely You are tired of hearing my woes on this subject. Maybe so tired that You decided to answer my prayer for our family. Thank You that as I put my head on my pillow tonight, I am feeling relaxed, thankful and in awe of Your marvelous ways. We needed $500 to make a dental payment, due the end of the week, and today You delivered a check for Tim's sales commission—the one we were sure had died in the process. We had both given up, but obviously You had not. Maybe You even held on to the money so that we'd have it at the right time for the right use. But I don't have to figure all that out. I just want to thank You for taking care of us, for loving us and for meeting our every need.

Action

List the blessings you received today and then give thanks to God in your own words.

Reflection

Good night, dear God. I love You, and I know that You love me.

Inspiration

"Living in the moment brings you a sense of reverence for all of life's blessings."

—Oprah Winfrey

Giving Thanks for a Problem Resolved

Dear Lord, I was so afraid this morning. I felt as though I had the weight of the world on my shoulders. Problems with kids and work and health and . . . well . . . you know the list better than I do! But what really mattered today was having to come to a decision about whether to continue working. Now that our children are teenagers, I want to be home more so that I can stay in touch with them and their friends and make sure we are talking every day. Yet I love my job, and we can sure use my salary. I prayed and You gave me the ideal solution. I can work from home. It sounded like an outlandish idea, but when I presented it to my supervisor, she was open to discussing it. Later she came to me with a big smile and thumbs up! It made sense to her. There's no reason I can't complete all my work at home and send it in electronically. In fact, it's good for the department, too. There will be more space and additional equipment for others to use. Thank You for helping me resolve this problem so effortlessly and for the benefit of everyone involved.

Action

Write down a problem you have faced and resolved. Then compose your own original prayer of thanks for the solution you received.

Reflection

Good night, dear God. I love you, and I know that you love me.

Inspiration

"A problem is a chance for you to do your best."

—Duke Ellington

LET ME UNDERSTAND THE TEACHING OF YOUR PRECEPTS;
THEN I WILL MEDITATE ON YOUR WONDERS.
PSALM 119:27

Giving Thanks for a Lesson Learned

Dear God, it is just plain hard to learn some of the lessons You have to teach me—such as this morning when I realized that I was being bossy and controlling again. I guess I still think I'm right most of the time! You've brought me to my knees more than once on this issue, and there I was, at it again—playing God in my husband's life. I seem to think if I just say what I have to say one more time, one more way, he will *get* it. But today You showed me clearly that *I'm* the one who doesn't get it. I'm the one who is driving us apart by micromanaging everything he does. Len finally told me he feels like a little kid when I talk to him as though he doesn't know how to manage his own affairs. What a shock! I thought I was being a good wife, a caring partner. All I did was remind him to take his vitamins, that blue socks don't go with black slacks, to drop his shirts at the laundry and . . . You're right! You're God and I'm not. Thank You for helping me learn this lesson one more time. Please make it stick this time.

Action

Think of at least one foolish choice you made today or one mistake that you now regret. Ask the Lord to show you the lesson. Learn it and move on.

Reflection

Good night, dear God. I love You, and I know that You love me.

Inspiration

"A life spent making mistakes is not only more honorable, but more useful than a life spent doing nothing."

—George Bernard Shaw

Giving Thanks for a Decision Made

Dear God, decisions, decisions—they are so challenging to make alone. I'm thankful that because of my relationship with You, I don't have to. I can turn to You in every situation and trust that You will be my guide and my guardian. I don't want to choose hastily, out of fear or worry or anxiety about what someone else might think of me. I want to do what is right in Your eyes for me at this time in my life. I remember my older friend Grace telling me the importance of listening to *You*. Sometimes another person may be the messenger, but if that is the case, You will confirm that in my spirit. Today there will be small and large decisions in front of me—details with our children, with a work project, with my neighbor who needs some help. I don't have the wisdom or strength in my own power to accomplish any of this. So now, as I lie down to sleep, I praise and thank You for leading me every time I must decide. I trust You and I bless Your holy name.

Action

What decision did you make today that you are proud of? Note it down on paper or type it into your computer. Keep track of all your successes from this day on. Then give God all the glory.

Reflection

Good night, dear God. I love You, and I know that You love me.

Inspiration

"Good plans shape good decisions. That's why good planning helps to make elusive dreams come true."

—Lester R. Bittel

MAY THE FAVOR OF THE LORD OUR GOD REST UPON US; ESTABLISH THE WORK OF OUR HANDS FOR US—YES, ESTABLISH THE WORK OF OUR HANDS.
PSALM 90:17

Giving Thanks for a Request Granted

Dear God, I am feeling extra grateful tonight. I asked You for favor today and You granted it. I am so relieved. I really needed to hear from You and You came through. It was as though I had a private line from my home to Yours! But then I do. You have told me again and again through Scripture that I am the apple of Your eye, Your beloved child, Your daughter and princess. When I come to You with concerns and doubts or a special need that I cannot meet in my own strength, there You are, leading me down the path of righteousness, providing me with answers I had not even imagined. How I do praise You for Your mercy and compassion! When things are tough for me, You soften them with Your wisdom and grace and loving-kindness. Thank You.

Action

How has God answered your prayers today? Consider His faithfulness to you. Write in your journal or diary a prayer of thanks.

Reflection

Good night, Lord. I love You, and I know that You love me.

Inspiration

"Ask questions from your heart and you will be answered from the heart."

—Omaha Proverb

OTHER BOOKS BY
Karen O'Connor

Help, Lord! I'm Having a Senior Moment
Notes to God on Growing Older

Help, Lord! I'm Having a Senior Moment—Again!
Laughing Through the Realities of Growing Older

More Moments with Karen O'Connor

Like it or not, senior moments happen. We might as well laugh about them and thank God for the way they add interest to our lives. After all, what would life be without the cordless phone ringing faintly from where you left it in the fridge?

Some senior moments are more heartbreaking or embarrassing than funny. But in every case, we can take them to the Lord who cares for us.

Help, Lord! I'm Having a Senior Moment
Notes to God on Growing Older
Karen O'Connor
ISBN 08307.34406

Help, Lord! I'm Having a Senior Moment—Again!
Laughing Through the Realities of Growing Older
Karen O'Connor
ISBN 08307.37081

"Karen has hit upon the things we least enjoy about getting older, but she enables us to see God's hand in our 'maturity.' . . . Now if I could just remember where I put my keys, I would drive to the store for more copies of this wonderful book for my friends!"

—Kathy Collard Miller
Women's Conference Speaker and Author of *Why Do I Put So Much Pressure on Myself?*

Available at Bookstores Everywhere!

Visit **www.regalbooks.com** to join **Regal's FREE e-newsletter.** You'll get useful **excerpts from our newest releases** and **special access to online chats with your favorite authors.** Sign up today!

God's Word for Your World™
www.regalbooks.com

Inspiring Reading for Women

Moments Together for Couples
Daily Devotions for Drawing Near to God and One Another
Dennis and Barbara Rainey
ISBN 08307.17544

Release the Pain, Embrace the Joy
Help for the Hurting Heart
Michelle McKinney Hammond
ISBN 08307.37227

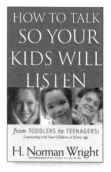

How to Talk So Your Kids Will Listen
From Toddlers to Teenagers—Connecting with Your Children at Every Age
H. Norman Wright
ISBN 08307.33280

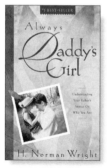

Always Daddy's Girl
Understanding Your Father's Impact on Who You Are
H. Norman Wright
ISBN 08307.27620

A Garden of Friends
How Friendships Enhance Every Season of Life
Penny Pierce Rose
ISBN 08307.37065

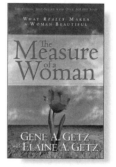

The Measure of a Woman
What Really Makes a Woman Beautiful
Gene A. Getz with Elaine Getz
ISBN 08307.32861